CAMBRIDGE
UNIVERSITY PRESS

Cambridge Grammar and Writing Skills

Learner's Book 9

Mike Gould and Eoin Higgins

Contents

Unit	Text type	Task type (aim)	Grammar	
1 People pointers	Story/narrative	To improve characterisation in imaginative writing	Gerunds and infinitives	
2 Selling a lifestyle	Advertisement	To create an advertisement that shows your persuasion skills	Adverbs to modify verbs and adjectives	
3 Natural encounters	Travel/descriptive writing	To shape language to evoke a real-life situation	Questions	
4 Listen up	Review	To write an effective review that is suitable for a particular audience	Present tenses: simple and perfect	
5 Past reflections	Personal writing/autobiography	To write effective and interesting commentaries	Past tenses	
6 Between the lines	Narrative/diary	To tell a narrative in an original way	Pronouns: indefinite, relative, demonstrative	
7 More than a play	Drama/play script	To use dramatic structure to create impact	Conditional sentences	
8 Making yourself heard	Persuasive speech/argument with linked progression	To write a speech for a specified audience	Making suggestions	
9 Writing about poetry	Poem/responding to a poem	To write a thoughtful response to a poem	Adverbs	
10 Family journeys	Descriptive writing	To write a story with a powerful description of place and people	Participles	
11 Explaining events	News report	To write an article about an aspect of a different culture	Subordinate clauses	
12 Finding freedom	Third person narratives	To write a powerful story about someone on their own	Continuous tenses: active and passive	

How to use this book

Unit walkthrough

The aim shows you the type of writing that you will look at in this unit.

Here you can see your objectives for this unit if you are a first language English learner.

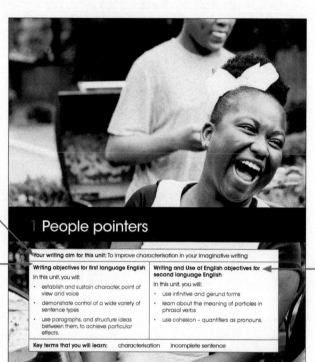

1 People pointers

Your writing aim for this unit: To improve characterisation in your imaginative writing

Writing objectives for first language English	Writing and Use of English objectives for second language English
In this unit, you will:	In this unit, you will:
• establish and sustain character, point of view and voice	• use infinitive and gerund forms
• demonstrate control of a wide variety of sentence types	• learn about the meaning of particles in phrasal verbs
• use paragraphs, and structure ideas between them, to achieve particular effects.	• use cohesion – quantifiers as pronouns.

Key terms that you will learn: characterisation   Incomplete sentence

If you are a second language English learner, you can see your objectives for the unit here.

Each unit begins with a 'Big Question'. This helps you to think about any knowledge you already have on the themes and subject of this unit.

This lists the main features found in an effective example of this type of writing.

The unit is divided into five sections. The first section is called 'Reading'. It focuses on a text extract that is typical of the type of writing covered by this unit. Texts include literature.

How do I convey character effectively through speech and action?

There is a phrase, 'actions speak louder than words'. Some people do good deeds (for example, doing charitable work) but don't boast or make a fuss about it. Equally, some people promise to do something and then do not stick to their words! Can you think of people like this? Friends or relatives who just help others or work hard without making a fuss? Or can you think of a time when you promised to do something but were unable to fulfil your promise?

Effective characterisation
A good narrative built around character should:

• show the main character's *speech* or *actions*

• show *how others react* or *respond* to the main character

• *allow the reader to draw conclusions* about what sort of person he/she is

• often show the main character in some sort of *conflict* or *dilemma*.

Glossary

conflict: a fight or disagreement

dilemma: a difficult decision faced by someone

Reading

The following extract concerns a young man named Bronze, who has not spoken a word since a terrifying fire in his village when he was a little child. All through the year, he has been going to the local town to sell beautiful shoes made from reeds, but now the winter has come. It is snowing and no one seems interested at first.

1 As you read the text, think about these questions:

a How does the author convey Bronze's character?

b What is the dilemma or problem Bronze has to face towards the end of the extract?

Key language features

verb patterns
phrasal verbs
quantifiers as pronouns

The Shoe Boy

Bronze didn't think these city people would be interested in buying reed shoes. After all, city people had cotton-padded shoes or leather shoes. So, he didn't beckon them over.

He was right. These city people didn't wear reed shoes, but when they came past him some of them stopped. The others wondered why, and stopped too. One or two of them must have been artists. They were enchanted by the ten pairs of fluffy reed shoes in the white light of the snow. The artists saw beauty – an extraordinary beauty – in these shoes. It was difficult to explain. One by one they stepped closer and touched the shoes – and when they touched them, they liked them even more. Some of them held them up to their noses and sniffed, a whiff of straw, which was especially strong in the cold air around them.

"They'd look so good on the wall at home," one of them said.

The others nodded and reached to grab a pair, afraid of missing out. There were nine in the group. They each took a pair, and one person took two. All ten were in their hands. Until they asked the price, Bronze wasn't at all sure that they were really going to buy them. He told them his price – the price that never changed. So cheap! thought the city people, and they handed over their money. They were delighted with their purchases, which they would take back to the city, and took great pleasure in examining them as they walked on.

Bronze stood there in the snow with a handful of cash. He'd done it! Then someone yelled from across the road, "Hey, mute, best get home now your shoes are sold! You'll freeze to death out here!"

Keep these questions in mind when you are reading the text for the first time. They help you to see the purpose behind what you are reading.

Coloured words in the text and the 'Key language features' box relate to English language terms that you will learn about later in the unit.

This list helps you to develop an appreciation of the type of text that you have just read.

Authentic texts are more challenging than those typically found in an ESL course.

The Teacher's Resource includes work on writers' effects.

'Glossary' boxes help to explain difficult or unusual words or phrases in the text. They are highlighted in red.

How the text works

Do you remember what makes good characterisation? Here is how the writer makes it work. He:

- reveals Bronze's thoughts and feelings directly ('He wasn't sure...')
- conveys Bronze's feelings indirectly through his actions ('He smiled...')
- shows us how others react to him (for example, the 'crowd of people')
- makes us think about Bronze's dilemma through the situation or events of the story (selling shoes outside in the winter).

> **Glossary**
>
> mute: someone who cannot speak
> Nainai: Bronze's grandmother
> warbled: sang in a high voice
> jabbed: hit forcefully and quickly, with a thin object

> **Key term**
>
> characterisation: the way people are presented in a book, poem, play or on screen

Bronze stuffed the cash into his inside pocket, untied the rope from the trees and fastened it round his waist. He looked across the road. There was a crowd of people watching him. He waved to them, and started running off through the snow like a madman.

The sky was clear and everything was bright. Bronze took the usual road home. He wanted to sing, to sing the song that Nainai sang when she was twisting rope. He couldn't sing out loud, so he sang in his head:

"Fishing for prawns in trees? Oh, put away your net!
Looking for gold in mud? There's only sand as yet!
Oranges grow on the black locust tree
Oh, when will we see the pe-o-ny!"

Someone was following him.

"Hey, shoe-boy, stop!"

Bronze stopped and glanced around warily. He didn't recognise the man and was suspicious. When the man caught up with Bronze, he said, "I saw them buying your shoes. Have you got any more? I'd like some too."

Bronze shook his head, and felt a bit sorry for him. The man wrung his hands, and sighed in disappointment. Bronze looked at him, and wished he could do something. The man turned and headed towards the pier, and Bronze turned and headed for home. After a while Bronze slowed down. He saw the reed shoes on his feet. He heard the snow crunch beneath them. He stopped walking, looked up at the sky, then down at the snow and, finally, at the reed shoes, which felt warm and snug on his feet. Nainai's song warbled through his mind. After a moment or two, he pulled his right foot out of his shoe and put it down on the snow. The cold jabbed like a needle. He did the same with his left. Immediately, the cold shot through his bones. He bent forward, picked up the shoes and held them up to inspect them. They'd

only been worn once in the snow and there were no dirty marks on them. They looked like new.

Bronze smiled, then turned and ran after the man. His bare feet sent snow spraying as they hit the ground. The man was stepping down to the pier to catch the steamboat when Bronze appeared in front of him, holding up the pair of reed shoes. The man couldn't believe his luck, and reached out to take them. He wanted to pay Bronze extra, but Bronze would only take his usual price.

Bronze waved at his last customer, then headed for home. He ran all the way, without once looking back. His feet were washed clean by the snow but were frozen red. Bright, bright red.

From *Bronze and Sunflower* by Cao Wenxuan

'Text analysis' is the second section of the unit. Here you will learn about the structure of the type of text that you have just read.

The activities in this section will break down the text into paragraphs and individual words, and help you to analyse them.

Text analysis

Good characterisation often depends on empathy. This is when readers become interested in a character because they can understand and sympathise with their situation. This is sometimes expressed as 'being in their shoes' (which is very suitable in this story!).

> **Glossary**
>
> empathy: being able to understand someone's situation or feelings

1 What things or aspects of the story help us to empathise with Bronze? (Think about his worries, the weather, etc.)

Reading closely

2 This part of the story hinges around two potential problems Bronze faces.

  a Why would 'city people' be interested in Bronze's village shoes?

  b What is the second problem, or dilemma, *after* he has sold the shoes and sets off home?

3 The first part of the extract is structured around the city people looking at the shoes.

  a Why does Bronze at first think they wouldn't be interested in his shoes?

  b How do the city people show, through their actions, that they are interested in buying them?

  c What do they intend to do with the shoes?

4 The second part of the extract is built around the dilemma Bronze faces as he walks home.

  a What does the man call Bronze when he stops him? What is Bronze's initial reaction?

  b How does the man react when Bronze shakes his head?

  c When does Bronze decide to give the man his own shoes – at that point, or later?

5 You will encounter stories with much more demanding vocabulary later in this Learner's Book, but part of this story's success is that it has an almost fairy tale simplicity.

The fairy tale style of the story is partly created by the city people's reaction to the shoes.

Which words or phrases in the second paragraph mean:

  a spellbound?

  b extreme loveliness?

  c hard to describe?

First screenshot (page 13)

6 The writer uses a number of short, simple sentences to convey Bronze's feelings or stress what has happened to him.

a At the start, the extract states: 'He was right.' What was Bronze 'right' about?

b Later, after the city people had gone, the extract states: 'He'd done it!'

  i What had he 'done'?

  ii Why do you think the writer uses this emphatic, short sentence with an exclamation mark?

c The extract ends with a phrase – a sort of incomplete sentence: 'Bright, bright red.' Why does the writer end like this? Consider these options (more than one might be right):

  • to explain that Bronze's feet are bleeding

  • to emphasise how cold Bronze's feet must be

  • to emphasise Bronze's kindness and unselfishness

  • to emphasise how far Bronze would go to help his family

  • to show how warm his feet are.

Key term

incomplete sentence: often this is a minor sentence that is missing the usual subject plus verb structure. For example, imperatives such as 'Go!' or answers to questions might not have the usual sentence parts. 'Bright, bright red' has no subject or verb, but could stand for 'They were bright, bright red.'

Thinking about the text

What are the 'pointers' that help readers to understand characters? It can be how the character acts or behaves, or how others respond to them.

7 Think carefully and then answer these questions.

a The writer uses the simile 'the cold jabbed like a needle' to describe how Bronze feels when he removes the shoes. What do the words 'jabbed' and 'needle' suggest about what he feels?

b A person calls Bronze 'mute' rather than by his name. How does that make you feel as a reader?

c What evidence is there at the end of the extract that the man at the pier appreciates Bronze's sacrifice?

React to the text

8 Work in pairs. Discuss these questions.

a In the story, Bronze has to stand out in very cold weather trying to sell his shoes. Have you ever had to do a job or wait around in extremely cold weather? How did you feel? Did you want to 'give up' and go inside?

b Why do you think Bronze decides to sell his own shoes to the man? How would you feel if you were in the same situation – would you have done the same?

c In what ways is the extract successful at building a picture of what Bronze is like through 'people pointers' such as how he behaves and how others react to him? Note down three ways.

Unit 1 People pointers **13**

Second screenshot (page 14)

Use of English

Later in the unit you are going to write part of a story about a character.

Gerunds and infinitives

Grammar presentation

In stories it is important to vary the language to keep the reader's attention, so writers often use a wide variety of verb patterns.

1 Match the sentence parts from the story on pages 10–11 to the verb patterns.

a ...people would be *interested in buying* reed shoes.	**i** verb + infinitive
b It was *difficult to explain*.	**ii** verb + gerund
c He *wanted to sing*...	**iii** infinitive of purpose
d He *stopped walking*, looked up at the sky...	**iv** preposition + gerund
e The others nodded and reached *to grab* a pair.	**v** adjective + infinitive

Find more examples of each pattern from Activity 1 in the story.

2 Verbs of the senses are followed by the gerund or the infinitive without *to*, depending on the meaning. Study these examples.

  She saw them **buying** your shoes.

The action was in progress when she saw it.

  He heard the snow **crunch** beneath them.

A short action that he heard from beginning to end.

3 Choose the correct verb form for each sentence.

a Chen turned around and saw a large man *walk / walking* towards him.

b Azra put her hand out *to take / taking* the money.

c They were tired of *to wait / waiting* around in the cold.

d Sanjay was too shy *to interrupt / interrupting* the conversation.

e I don't mind *to leave / leaving* a little later if you can't now.

f They didn't appear *to be / being* eager *to continue / continuing*.

4 Complete the story extract with the correct form of the verbs in brackets.

Meera heard a voice (a) _____ (call) her but she refused (b) _____ (turn) around. Her friend kept (c) _____ (talk) so Meera focused all her attention on (d) _____ (listen) to Tara's long rant about how impossible it was (e) _____ (study) in the library with all the noise. But it was no use. The voice got more difficult (f) _____ (ignore) and Meera decided (g) _____ (glance) around quickly ... she was delighted (h) _____ (see) it was someone she knew.

14 Unit 1 People pointers

Callout boxes

'Key term' boxes highlight new or important language that you will work on in the unit.

These discussion questions let you talk about your personal reaction to the text and add your own thoughts.

The 'Use of English' section looks at grammar or vocabulary in relation to the text type.

First of all, you will read about the new grammar or vocabulary in one of these presentation boxes.

You will be asked to actively think about the grammar rules and use.

This is followed by lots of activities to help you practise the new language.

Each unit includes one grammar box and one vocabulary box.

Helpful 'Tips' relating to grammar and writing can be found in each unit.

You may also find an extra presentation box focusing on punctuation or cohesion. This information will help you to write better texts.

Vocabulary: phrasal verb particles

Vocabulary presentation

Certain movements or actions can only be described using phrasal verbs. In descriptive language in stories, phrasal verbs can be very useful. Often the meaning of the particle can help you to understand what the phrasal verb means.

5 Look at the following phrasal verbs from the story on pages 10–11. What do the particles mean?

a Some of them held them *up* to their noses…

b …they handed *over* their money.

c …took great pleasure in examining them as they walked *on*.

d He waved to them, and started running *off*…

e The man couldn't believe his luck, and reached *out* to take them.

6 Choose the correct particle to complete each sentence.

a All lifted *up* / *off* the box to check how heavy it was.

b Instead of stopping the car, she just drove *up* / *on*.

c Diya stepped *around* / *over* the puddle but Shyla jumped right into it.

d Aulia caught *up* / *on* with Rafi to ask him for help, but he just walked *up* / *off*.

e We slowed *off* / *down* to let some sheep cross the road. Then they all ran *away* / *over* across the fields.

Tip

Understanding the different meanings of prepositions and particles can really help you to learn phrasal verbs.

7 Complete the story extract with the correct particles.

Chang didn't know whether to ride
(a) _____ or stop to help the old woman who had obviously fallen
(b) _____. In the end, he pulled
(c) _____ on his bike, hopped
(d) _____ and laid his bike
(e) _____ on the ground. The woman looked (f) _____ at Chang and held (g) _____ her hand. Chang pulled her (h) _____ and she began to walk (i) _____ without saying anything. Just as Chang was about to ride (j) _____ on his bike, the woman turned (k) _____ and called (l) _____ to Chang. 'Thank you, little girl,' she said and smiled.

Cohesion: quantifiers as pronouns

Cohesion presentation

Sometimes we can use quantifiers (*some, any, many, a few,* etc.) as pronouns when it is clear what they are referring to.

8 What do the quantifiers in bold in this sentence refer to?
*"I saw them buying your shoes. Have you got **any more**? I'd like **some** too."*

9 Cross out the words that are not needed in each sentence.

a Mrs Zhang offered some cake but I didn't want any more cake.

b There were boys standing around the door. Some of the boys were laughing.

c A bowl of sugar was placed in front of Hana. She put some sugar in her tea.

d People started to run in all directions. Many people took shelter in the shops and a few people stood under the tree.

Unit 1 People pointers 15

'Guided writing' is the fourth section. This will guide you step-by-step through a writing activity that is related to the text type.

You will be presented with a model task to complete.

The first step is to brainstorm and plan ideas for your writing.

This will include opportunities to plan collaboratively with other students.

Helpful 'Tips' relating to grammar and writing can be found in each unit.

'Useful language' boxes provide words and phrases that will help with your writing.

You will work intensively on writing just one part of the text type.

Guided writing

You have decided to enter a story competition with a story using the following title: 'The Outsider'.

Create an extract from a story, written in the third person, in which a character from one community or place is in a strange or very different place. Your character has to face some sort of problematic situation or dilemma, and describe how other people react to him or her.

Write an extract from a story for the competition.

Think/Plan

Work in pairs. Generate ideas about your main character. Answer the questions to help you.

a Why is your character considered an 'outsider'?

b What is his/her name? What does he/she look like?

c Does he/she have any distinguishing features?

Tip

You could use a mind map to generate ideas for your story. Use the questions to help you.

16 Unit 1 People pointers

2 Now organise your story. Think about the setting, the main events, and the outcome. Discuss these questions with a partner.

a Where does the story take place? What is the situation?

b What dilemma does the character face?

c How does the character resolve the situation?

Useful language

Phrases: *[character] didn't think that…, After all, …, [character] wasn't at all sure that…, He/She didn't recognise…, …was suspicious, …felt a bit sorry for…, …wished he/she could do something.*

Gerunds and infinitives: *It was difficult/ easy to…, He/She was too shy to…, He/She wanted to…, X didn't appear to…, X was tired of …ing, X seemed interested in …ing, X heard/saw him/her …ing, He/She stopped …ing*

Phrasal verbs (actions): *hold up/lift up, hand over/step over, walk on/drive on, run off, reach out, catch up with, slow down, run away*

Write: the build-up

The story about Bronze on pages 10–11 starts by presenting a situation in which the main character seems to have come out very well, despite his first impression.

Write the first part of your story.

a First, think about the build-up to the dilemma. Here are some ideas:

• X was sure she going in the right direction.

• X was excited to be putting on his new school uniform for the first time.

• It had been a delicious lunch and X felt great.

Create an atmosphere, with details about the place, the weather, the people, the action, etc.

Write: first paragraph

Write the first paragraph of your review.

Include the following information:

- the name of the band and the album
- the release date and the time since the band's last album
- the number of tracks
- potential audience/appeal.

You should also write a headline and a subtitle.

Write: main body

Write the main body of your review.

Describe some stand-out tracks or aspects of the album. Include information about the music, lyrics, style and content, and use interesting adjectives to describe these aspects. Write two or three paragraphs.

a Use the present perfect simple to explain the background to the track.

b Use the present simple to comment on the different aspects of the track.

c Show your knowledge of music: instruments, styles, production, etc.

Did you know?

Reviewers often pack a lot of information into the sentences in the main body. Look at this example from the review on pages 40–41.

Suga, who has often proven his skill at writing melancholy lyrics, does it again in Trivia: Seesaw, a fizzy, synthesiser-driven number that charts the end of a relationship.

style and content

background information

Write: conclusion

Now write the conclusion of your review.

Use the final paragraph to comment on the future of the band, album and/or genre. Here are some ideas to help you.

- *This album will surely consolidate…*
- *This new material will definitely appeal to…*
- *It may not be their best material so far, but it will…*
- *Perhaps this new album will help to put [band] on the international stage.*

Things to remember when writing a review

- Write about something relevant at the time of writing.
- Match the style and language to your audience.
- Demonstrate your knowledge of the topic through the vocabulary.
- Give a strong viewpoint in an entertaining way.
- Use the present perfect to explain the background.
- Use the present simple to comment on what you are reviewing.

Check your first draft

When you have finished writing your review, share it with your partner.

a Check that your partner has included all of the correct information.

b Pay attention to whether his/her opinions are clear and consistent.

c Assess whether the style and language are appropriate for the type of reader.

Peer assessment

Decide on a set of criteria for your partner to use to evaluate your work.

Now write a second draft of your review.

'Things to remember' offers a reminder of the important points that you should cover in your writing.

The unit includes opportunities for self-assessment. This will help you to develop responsibility for your own learning.

You will also learn to edit and then redraft your own writing.

Useful facts relating to the text type or writing can be found in the 'Did you know?' boxes.

The 'Peer assessment' boxes allow you to collaborate with other students and reflect on each other's work.

Independent writing

Write a story of 300–350 words that conveys a character.

Choose one of these ideas for a character or use your own.

- Honey didn't mind that everyone was taller than her.
- Alpin always wore a red woolly hat.
- Junko walked out of the sea back to the beach. It was colder today.

Follow these stages.

Stage 1 Generate ideas for your character. Think about: what he/she looks like; how he/she dresses; how he/she speaks and moves.

Stage 2 Put your ideas into a mind map.

- Where will your story take place? What situation does your main character find himself/herself in?
- What dilemma does he/she face?
- How does it all end?

Stage 3 Write your story in paragraphs, following your plan. Use the checklist to make sure your story is full of suspense.

Writer's checklist: conveying character

- Have you created an interesting character?
- Have you conveyed your character through their speech and actions?
- Have you created a dilemma for your character?
- Have you used a variety of sentence structures to create different effects?
- Have you made the reader think about the character through the situation and events?
- Have you used phrasal verbs for different actions?

Editor's checklist

Check

- that your ideas are organised into paragraphs
- your spelling and use of capital letters
- punctuation
- the grammar is correct – phrasal verbs, gerunds and infinitives.

Final draft

Once you have completed your story, post it on the wall in your class or on your class website. Invite readers to comment on it.

Check your progress

I can:	Needs more work	Almost there	All done!
develop and convey a character through speech and actions			
create a dilemma for a character to face and resolve			
use a variety of short and long sentences to build tension			
reveal the character's feelings through their actions.			

'Independent writing' is the final section. Using all the information that you have learnt in the unit, you can now complete an entire writing activity on your own.

The word limit for your writing activity is provided.

Each writing activity has a choice of tasks. This will help you to access the right one for you.

The unit ends with a progress checklist where you can reflect on your own learning.

The 'Writer's checklist' is a final reminder of what you covered in the unit and what you should include in your writing.

The 'Editor's checklist' is a final reminder of how to edit and proofread your writing.

'Final draft' suggests what you or your whole class can do with your finished writing.

1 People pointers

Your writing aim for this unit: To improve characterisation in your imaginative writing

Writing objectives for first language English

In this unit, you will:

- establish and sustain character, point of view and voice

- demonstrate control of a wide variety of sentence types

- use paragraphs, and structure ideas between them, to achieve particular effects.

Writing and Use of English objectives for second language English

In this unit, you will:

- use infinitive and gerund forms

- learn about the meaning of particles in phrasal verbs

- use cohesion – quantifiers as pronouns.

Key terms that you will learn: characterisation   incomplete sentence

How do I convey character effectively through speech and action?

There is a phrase, 'actions speak louder than words'. Some people do good deeds (for example, doing charitable work) but don't boast or make a fuss about it. Equally, some people promise to do something and then do not stick to their words! Can you think of people like this? Friends or relatives who just help others or work hard without making a fuss? Or can you think of a time when you promised to do something but were unable to fulfil your promise?

Effective characterisation

A good narrative built around character should:

- show the main character's *speech* or *actions*

- show *how others react* or *respond* to the main character

- *allow the reader to draw conclusions* about what sort of person he/she is

- often show the main character in some sort of **conflict** or **dilemma**.

Glossary

conflict: a fight or disagreement

dilemma: a difficult decision faced by someone

Reading

The following extract concerns a young man named Bronze, who has not spoken a word since a terrifying fire in his village when he was a little child. All through the year, he has been going to the local town to sell beautiful shoes made from reeds, but now the winter has come. It is snowing and no one seems interested at first.

1 As you read the text, think about these questions:

a How does the author convey Bronze's character?

b What is the dilemma or problem Bronze has to face towards the end of the extract?

Key language features

verb patterns
phrasal verbs
quantifiers as pronouns

The Shoe Boy

Bronze didn't think these city people would be interested in buying reed shoes. After all, city people had cotton-padded shoes or leather shoes. So, he didn't beckon them over.

He was right. These city people didn't wear reed shoes, but when they came past him some of them stopped. The others wondered why, and stopped too. One or two of them must have been artists. They were enchanted by the ten pairs of fluffy reed shoes in the white light of the snow. The artists saw beauty – an extraordinary beauty – in these shoes. It was difficult to explain. One by one they stepped closer and touched the shoes – and when they touched them, they liked them even more. Some of them held them up to their noses and sniffed, a whiff of straw, which was especially strong in the cold air around them.

"They'd look so good on the wall at home," one of them said.

The others nodded and reached to grab a pair, afraid of missing out. There were nine in the group. They each took a pair, and one person took two. All ten were in their hands. Until they asked the price, Bronze wasn't at all sure that they were really going to buy them. He told them his price – the price that never changed. So cheap! thought the city people, and they handed over their money. They were delighted with their purchases, which they would take back to the city, and took great pleasure in examining them as they walked on.

Bronze stood there in the snow with a handful of cash. He'd done it! Then someone yelled from across the road, "Hey, **mute**, best get home now your shoes are sold! You'll freeze to death out here!"

How the text works

Do you remember what makes good **characterisation**? Here is how the writer makes it work. He:

- reveals Bronze's thoughts and feelings directly ('He wasn't sure…')
- conveys Bronze's feelings indirectly through his actions ('He smiled…')
- shows us how others react to him (for example, the 'crowd of people')
- makes us think about Bronze's dilemma through the situation or events of the story (selling shoes outside in the winter).

Bronze stuffed the cash into his inside pocket, untied the rope from the trees and fastened it round his waist. He looked across the road. There was a crowd of people watching him. He waved to them, and started running off through the snow like a madman.

The sky was clear and everything was bright. Bronze took the usual road home. He wanted to sing, to sing the song that **Nainai** sang when she was twisting rope. He couldn't sing out loud, so he sang in his head:

"Fishing for prawns in trees? Oh, put away your net!
Looking for gold in mud? There's only sand as yet!
Oranges grow on the black locust tree
Oh, when will we see the pe-o-ny?"

Someone was following him.

"Hey, shoe-boy, stop!"

Bronze stopped and glanced around warily. He didn't recognise the man and was suspicious. When the man caught up with Bronze, he said, "I saw them buying your shoes. Have you got any more? I'd like some too."

Bronze shook his head, and felt a bit sorry for him. The man wrung his hands, and sighed in disappointment. Bronze looked at him, and wished he could do something. The man turned and headed towards the pier, and Bronze turned and headed for home. After a while Bronze slowed down. He saw the reed shoes on his feet. He heard the snow crunch beneath them. He stopped walking, looked up at the sky, then down at the snow and, finally, at the reed shoes, which felt warm and snug on his feet. Nainai's song **warbled** through his mind. After a moment or two, he pulled his right foot out of his shoe and put it down on the snow. The cold **jabbed** like a needle. He did the same with his left. Immediately, the cold shot through his bones. He bent forward, picked up the shoes and held them up to inspect them. They'd

only been worn once in the snow and there were no dirty marks on them. They looked like new.

Bronze smiled, then turned and ran after the man. His bare feet sent snow spraying as they hit the ground. The man was stepping down to the pier to catch the steamboat when Bronze appeared in front of him, holding up the pair of reed shoes. The man couldn't believe his luck, and reached out to take them. He wanted to pay Bronze extra, but Bronze would only take his usual price.

Bronze waved at his last customer, then headed for home. He ran all the way, without once looking back. His feet were washed clean by the snow but were frozen red. Bright, bright red.

From *Bronze and Sunflower* by Cao Wenxuan

Text analysis

Good characterisation often depends on **empathy**. This is when readers become interested in a character because they can understand and sympathise with their situation. This is sometimes expressed as 'being in their shoes' (which is very suitable in this story!).

> **Glossary**
>
> **empathy**: being able to understand someone's situation or feelings

1 What things or aspects of the story help us to empathise with Bronze? (Think about his worries, the weather, etc.)

Reading closely

2 This part of the story hinges around two potential problems Bronze faces.

a Why would 'city people' be interested in Bronze's village shoes?

b What is the second problem, or dilemma, *after* he has sold the shoes and sets off home?

3 The first part of the extract is structured around the city people looking at the shoes.

a Why does Bronze at first think they wouldn't be interested in his shoes?

b How do the city people show, through their actions, that they are interested in buying them?

c What do they intend to do with the shoes?

4 The second part of the extract is built around the dilemma Bronze faces as he walks home.

a What does the man call Bronze when he stops him? What is Bronze's initial reaction?

b How does the man react when Bronze shakes his head?

c When does Bronze decide to give the man his own shoes – at that point, or later?

5 You will encounter stories with much more demanding vocabulary later in this Learner's Book, but part of this story's success is that it has an almost fairy tale simplicity.

The fairy tale style of the story is partly created by the city people's reaction to the shoes.

Which words or phrases in the second paragraph mean:

a spellbound?

b extreme loveliness?

c hard to describe?

6 The writer uses a number of short, simple sentences to convey Bronze's feelings or stress what has happened to him.

    a At the start, the extract states: 'He was right.' What was Bronze 'right' about?

    b Later, after the city people had gone, the extract states: 'He'd done it!'

      i What had he 'done'?

      ii Why do you think the writer uses this emphatic, short sentence with an exclamation mark?

    c The extract ends with a phrase – a sort of **incomplete sentence**: 'Bright, bright red.' Why does the writer end like this? Consider these options (more than one might be right):

- to explain that Bronze's feet are bleeding

- to emphasise how cold Bronze's feet must be

- to emphasise Bronze's kindness and unselfishness

- to emphasise how far Bronze would go to help his family

- to show how warm his feet are.

Key term

incomplete sentence: often this is a minor sentence that is missing the usual subject plus verb structure. For example, imperatives such as 'Go!' or answers to questions might not have the usual sentence parts. 'Bright, bright red' has no subject or verb, but could stand for '*They were* bright, bright red.'

Thinking about the text

What are the 'pointers' that help readers to understand characters? It can be how the character acts or behaves, or how others respond to them.

7 Think carefully and then answer these questions.

    a The writer uses the simile 'the cold jabbed like a needle' to describe how Bronze feels when he removes the shoes. What do the words 'jabbed' and 'needle' suggest about what he feels?

    b A person calls Bronze 'mute' rather than by his name. How does that make you feel as a reader?

    c What evidence is there at the end of the extract that the man at the pier appreciates Bronze's sacrifice?

React to the text

8 Work in pairs. Discuss these questions.

    a In the story, Bronze has to stand out in very cold weather trying to sell his shoes. Have you ever had to do a job or wait around in extremely cold weather? How did you feel? Did you want to 'give up' and go inside?

    b Why do you think Bronze decides to sell his own shoes to the man? How would you feel if you were in the same situation – would you have done the same?

    c In what ways is the extract successful at building a picture of what Bronze is like through 'people pointers' such as how he behaves and how others react to him? Note down three ways.

Use of English

Later in the unit you are going to write part of a story about a character.

Gerunds and infinitives

Grammar presentation

In stories it is important to vary the language to keep the reader's attention, so writers often use a wide variety of verb patterns.

1 Match the sentence parts from the story on pages 10–11 to the verb patterns.

a ...people would be *interested in buying* reed shoes.	**i** verb + infinitive
b It was *difficult to explain.*	**ii** verb + gerund
c He *wanted to sing*...	**iii** infinitive of purpose
d He *stopped walking*, looked up at the sky...	**iv** preposition + gerund
e The others nodded and reached *to grab* a pair.	**v** adjective + infinitive

Find more examples of each pattern from Activity 1 in the story.

2 Verbs of the senses are followed by the gerund or the infinitive without *to*, depending on the meaning. Study these examples.

> *She saw them **buying** your shoes.*

The action was in progress when she saw it.

> *He heard the snow **crunch** beneath them.*

A short action that he heard from beginning to end.

3 Choose the correct verb form for each sentence.

a Chen turned around and saw a large man *walk / walking* towards him.

b Azra put her hand out *to take / taking* the money.

c They were tired of *to wait / waiting* around in the cold.

d Sanjay was too shy *to interrupt / interrupting* the conversation.

e I don't mind *to leave / leaving* a little later if you can't now.

f They didn't appear *to be / being* eager *to continue / continuing*.

4 Complete the story extract with the correct form of the verbs in brackets.

Meera heard a voice **(a)** _____ (call) her but she refused **(b)** _____ (turn) around. Her friend kept **(c)** _____ (talk) so Meera focused all her attention on **(d)** _____ (listen) to Tara's long rant about how impossible it was **(e)** _____ (study) in the library with all the noise. But it was no use. The voice got more difficult **(f)** _____ (ignore) and Meera decided **(g)** _____ (glance) around quickly ... she was delighted **(h)** _____ (see) it was someone she knew.

Vocabulary: phrasal verb particles

Certain movements or actions can only be described using phrasal verbs. In descriptive language in stories, phrasal verbs can be very useful. Often the meaning of the particle can help you to understand what the phrasal verb means.

5 Look at the following phrasal verbs from the story on pages 10–11. What do the particles mean?

   a Some of them held them *up* to their noses…

   b …they handed *over* their money.

   c …took great pleasure in examining them as they walked *on*.

   d He waved to them, and started running *off*…

   e The man couldn't believe his luck, and reached *out* to take them.

6 Choose the correct particle to complete each sentence.

   a Ali lifted *up / off* the box to check how heavy it was.

   b Instead of stopping the car, she just drove *up / on*.

   c Diya stepped *around / over* the puddle but Shyla jumped right into it.

   d Aulia caught *up / on* with Rafi to ask him for help, but he just walked *up / off*.

   e We slowed *off / down* to let some sheep cross the road. Then they all ran *away / over* across the fields.

Understanding the different meanings of prepositions and particles can really help you to learn phrasal verbs.

7 Complete the story extract with the correct particles.

Chang didn't know whether to ride (a) _____ or stop to help the old woman who had obviously fallen (b) _____. In the end, he pulled (c) _____ on his bike, hopped (d) _____ and laid his bike (e) _____ on the ground. The woman looked (f) _____ at Chang and held (g) _____ her hand. Chang pulled her (h) _____ and she began to walk (i) _____ without saying anything. Just as Chang was about to ride (j) _____ on his bike, the woman turned (k) _____ and called (l) _____ to Chang. 'Thank you, little girl,' she said and smiled.

Cohesion: quantifiers as pronouns

Sometimes we can use quantifiers (*some, any, many, a few,* etc.) as pronouns when it is clear what they are referring to.

8 What do the quantifiers in bold in this sentence refer to?

   *"I saw them buying your shoes. Have you got **any more**? I'd like **some** too."*

9 Cross out the words that are not needed in each sentence.

   a Mrs Zhang offered some cake but I didn't want any more cake.

   b There were boys standing around the door. Some of the boys were laughing.

   c A bowl of sugar was placed in front of Hana. She put some sugar in her tea.

   d People started to run in all directions. Many people took shelter in the shops and a few people stood under the tree.

Guided writing

You have decided to enter a story competition with a story using the following title: 'The Outsider'.

Create an extract from a story, written in the third person, in which a character from one community or place is in a strange or very different place. Your character has to face some sort of problematic situation or dilemma, and describe how other people react to him or her.

Write an extract from a story for the competition.

Think/Plan

1 Work in pairs. Generate ideas about your main character. Answer the questions to help you.

   a Why is your character considered an 'outsider'?

   b What is his/her name? What does he/she look like?

   c Does he/she have any distinguishing features?

Tip

You could use a mind map to generate ideas for your story. Use the questions to help you.

2 Now organise your story. Think about the setting, the main events, and the outcome. Discuss these questions with a partner.

   a Where does the story take place? What is the situation?

   b What dilemma does the character face?

   c How does the character resolve the situation?

Useful language

Phrases: *[character] didn't think that…, After all, …, [character] wasn't at all sure that…, He/She didn't recognise…, …was suspicious., …felt a bit sorry for…, …wished he/she could do something.*

Gerunds and infinitives: *It was difficult/ easy to…, He/She was too shy to…, He/She wanted to…, X didn't appear to…, X was tired of …ing, X seemed interested in …ing, X heard/saw him/her …ing, He/She stopped …ing*

Phrasal verbs (actions): *hold up/lift up, hand over/step over, walk on/drive on, run off, reach out, catch up with, slow down, run away*

Write: the build-up

The story about Bronze on pages 10–11 starts by presenting a situation in which the main character seems to have come out very well, despite his first impression.

Write the first part of your story.

a First, think about the build-up to the dilemma. Here are some ideas:

   • *X was sure she was going in the right direction.*

   • *X was excited to be putting on his new school uniform for the first time.*

   • *It had been a delicious lunch and X felt great.*

Create an atmosphere, with details about the place, the weather, the people, the action, etc.

b Hint at the fact that not everything is certain or that the main character is not completely in control. Introduce a note of doubt. For example:

- *Something didn't look right but X walked on.*

- *X was sure he had brought enough money...*

- *Everyone was walking in the same direction so X followed them.*

c Create a false sense of security. For example, Bronze runs home singing his favourite song after selling all the shoes.

Write: the dilemma

Present a problematic situation for the main character.

For example:

- *...couldn't find the...*

- *...found himself/herself completely lost...*

- *...now he/she was trapped...*

a Describe the causes of the problematic situation or dilemma.

b Use shorter sentences to increase the tension.

c Think about the choices the character could make.

Finish the story

Now write the end of your story. Explain what the character does to resolve the situation.

a Make the main character do something unexpected. There should be some sort of sacrifice and compromise.

b Describe the reaction of the other character(s).

c End by describing how the main character felt, and make us think about him/her.

Things to remember when conveying character

- Use speech and action for the character.

- Convey the character's feelings through actions.

- Show how others respond to the character.

- Use a variety of sentence lengths to build up tension.

- Make us reflect on the character.

Check your first draft

When you have finished writing, be your own editor.

a Now that you have completed your story and you have written the resolution, go back and read the story again more critically, to make sure that the build-up to the dilemma leads in well and presents a convincing character.

b Ask yourself if people will believe that your character is capable of doing what he/she did.

c Give your story to a partner and discuss the main character and his/her actions and speech.

Peer assessment

When you give your first draft to your partner, present it as neatly as possible to give a good first impression.

Now write a second draft of the story.

Independent writing

Write a story of 300–350 words that conveys a character.

Choose *one* of these ideas for a character or use your own.

- Honey didn't mind that everyone was taller than her.
- Alpin always wore a red woolly hat.
- Junko walked out of the sea back to the beach. It was colder today.

Follow these stages.

Stage 1 Generate ideas for your character. Think about: what he/she looks like; how he/she dresses; how he/she speaks and moves.

Stage 2 Put your ideas into a mind map.

- Where will your story take place? What situation does your main character find himself/herself in?
- What dilemma does he/she face?
- How does it all end?

Stage 3 Write your story in paragraphs, following your plan. Use the checklist to make sure your story is full of suspense.

Writer's checklist: conveying character

- Have you created an interesting character?
- Have you conveyed your character through their speech and actions?
- Have you created a dilemma for your character?
- Have you used a variety of sentence structures to create different effects?
- Have you made the reader think about the character through the situation and events?
- Have you used phrasal verbs for different actions?

Editor's checklist

Check

- that your ideas are organised into paragraphs
- your spelling and use of capital letters
- punctuation
- the grammar is correct – phrasal verbs, gerunds and infinitives.

Final draft

Once you have completed your story, post it on the wall in your class or on your class website. Invite readers to comment on it.

Check your progress

I can:	Needs more work	Almost there	All done!
develop and convey a character through speech and actions			
create a dilemma for a character to face and resolve			
use a variety of short and long sentences to build tension			
reveal the character's feelings through their actions.			

2 Selling a lifestyle

Your writing aim for this unit: To create an advertisement that shows your persuasion skills

Writing objectives for first language English	**Writing and Use of English objectives for second language English**
In this unit, you will:	In this unit, you will:
• link ideas and planning choices to a clear sense of task, purpose and audience	• use adverbs to modify verbs and adjectives
• write persuasively	• learn adjectives commonly used in advertising
• use a wide variety of sentence types.	• learn how to write effective headings.

Key terms that you will learn: advertisement   direct address

What techniques do I need to learn to write persuasively?

Imagine the humble pencil was a new invention that no one had ever seen. How would you advertise it? How would you describe its qualities and the benefits it would bring to someone's life? Spend one minute introducing 'the pencil' to a partner and trying to persuade them how wonderful it is. Then swap roles so your partner has a chance to do the selling. Begin

'I want to introduce you to something special. We call it "the pencil"...'

Effective advertisements for lifestyle products

A good **lifestyle advertisement** should:

- **promote** the benefits of the product or service to the reader or **consumer**

- *suggest a way of living* that is *attractive* to the consumer

- use *memorable images*, **logos** or **slogans**

- use a *variety of persuasive techniques* in the *structure* or choice of *language*.

Glossary

lifestyle: how people live (type of home, friends, job, etc.)

promote: support or praise a product/ service and its benefits

consumer: someone who buys or uses a product or service

logo: symbol or sign that shows what the brand is

slogan: a memorable statement or saying related to the product

Key term

advertisement: picture, text or short film that tries to persuade people to buy something or use a service

Reading

The following advertisement promotes a gadget that claims to help people take even better 'selfies'.

SMALL IS THE NEW BIG

LIBERATINGLY BOUNDLESS

LIFE-SIZE EMOTIONS

Your life. Your stories. Your way.

AirSelfie is about more than images. It's about giving you the most unique, flying camera technology to tell the world your story, exactly as you want to tell it. Discover breathtaking heights where the only limit is your imagination. Explore your world from an aerial perspective and unleash your personality.

NEAREST AND DEAREST
QUALITY TIME TOGETHER

Snap unforgettable moments with your friends and family. Take group selfies – groufies – from up to 20m away, capturing both your loved ones and the panorama. Perfect for an aerial group photo around a birthday cake or capturing the applause at your wedding. AirSelfie will change your photos forever.

LIFE IS A JOURNEY
VACATIONS BIG AND SMALL

Beach, mountain, city break, backpacking adventure. Take AirSelfie with you wherever you go. Achieve quirky, previously unseen angles of famous monuments, stunning aerial panoramas or just you and your friends having holiday fun. Then post your snap directly on social media, and make your friends wild with jealousy.

WE ARE WHAT WE LOVE
DEFINING DIVERTISSEMENTS

We've all got a passion. Something we love doing. Something that makes us us. AirSelfie lets you capture whatever that is in a way that is truly individual. Get your pal to snap you riding the waves from a bird's-eye perspective. Take a panoramic shot when you've successfully scaled that mountain. Show the world exactly how you checkmated your greatest chess adversary. Express your passion, your personality. With the best, boundless selfies captured from the air.

1 As you read the text, think about these questions:

a What, exactly, is the AirSelfie, and what does it do?

b Who do you think the advertisement is aimed at, given the use of images and what the text says?

Glossary

divertissements: French word meaning 'diversions' – things to take us away from everyday life

profile: your personal page with information about what you are doing

likes: (n) instant responses which tell you if someone likes what you've done or shown

IT'S WHAT'S ON THE INSIDE THAT COUNTS
THE GREAT INDOORS

The first portable flying camera is completely safe to use inside. Use AirSelfie to take previously unattainable wide-angle HD shots of special family dinners, cosy evenings cuddled up in front of the television, or the magic of a club night with friends. It's the first device you can truly make your own.

LIVE, SNAP, SHARE
SOCIAL MEDIA HAPPY

Live life to the fullest. Capture your story, your way, without bounds. And then share with the world. With AirSelfie you can post your snaps directly on Facebook, Instagram and Twitter with just the touch of a screen. Watch your **profiles** fill with amazing aerial shots, and let the **likes** roll in.

LOVE WORK
INNOVATE YOUR WORKING LIFE

Bring new perspectives to your work life with AirSelfie. Create a time-lapse of company event set-ups, fill your marketing messages with click-happy aerial images, show clients photos of your latest construction project, and much more. Whatever field of work you're in, the possibilities are as boundless as the sky.

How the text works

Do you remember what makes a good advertisement? Here is how the writer makes it work. He/she:

- structured the text to put across the main benefits of the product

- used images, headings and subheadings to draw the attention of the reader

- captured the reader's interest by using a range of language techniques (slogan, **direct address**, repetition, positive language, etc.)

- suggested a lifestyle the reader could be part of through lots of examples.

Key term

direct address: when the writer uses the second person ('you') form to the reader

Text analysis

1 How does the advertisement create an impact? Before you look at the content in detail, pick out two to three things that stand out or make you want to read more. Share those ideas with a partner – was their eye drawn to the same things?

Reading closely

2 The form and structure of the advertisement is partly why it is effective. Look at it again carefully, and use the table below to complete a report on how the advertisement is presented.

Try to say how each feature has been presented.

3 In an online advertisement, the most important and attention-grabbing information usually comes at the top.

  a Is this true in the case of the AirSelfie advertisement?

  b Why do you think this is the case?

4 There are six sections after the introductory one.

  a Which one suggests AirSelfie is great for travelling and holidays?

  b The third section is about pastimes. What three examples does the advertisement say AirSelfie could be used for?

  c How does the last sentence of the advertisement link with the first subheading/strapline under the title?

Feature	Example from the AirSelfie advertisement	How or where it is shown
Main slogan/heading	Small is the new big	Largest letters – at top of the advertisement
Subheading or strapline 1		
Subheading or strapline 2		
Image 1		
Image 2		
Section headings		
Section subheadings		
Anything else?		

5 The advertisement uses persuasive language in many different ways.

At various times, the language devices in the table below are used. Working in a small group, make sure you are clear what each one is – and then:

a divide up the devices (for example, 'direct address') among the group members

b find at least one (and possibly more) examples of the device you have been given

c make a note of why it might be effective and add it to a 'group grid' like the one below.

Thinking about the text

The various elements of an advertisement combine together to create a key message or set of messages to make the reader buy the product.

6 Think carefully and then answer the question.

What do you think the key messages of the advertisement are? Consider these options:

a This product is very cheap and good value.

b This product will fit in with a young, active and social lifestyle.

c This product is exclusive and only for the very rich.

d This product will help you sort out a problem in your life.

e This product will give you freedom to express yourself.

React to the text

7 Work in pairs. Discuss these questions.

a Is the AirSelfie a good idea? Can you think of any reasons why some people might *not* like it?

b How often (if at all) do you take selfies? In what situations?

c In what ways do you think the advertisement is effective in promoting the product? Think about:

i How you feel about the advertisement and the product

ii Why the advertisement makes you feel this (for example, does it make you want to share in the lifestyle shown? Is it something about the language you liked/disliked? Do you find out enough about the product? Is the advertisement presented effectively?)

Direct address – using 'you', 'your' etc. to 'speak' to the reader *Example:*	**Short phrases for impact** – sometimes with repeated words in them *Example:*	**Powerful adjectives** – for example, 'unforgettable' *Example:*
Imperative verbs – strong commands such as 'Get', 'Go', etc. *Example:*	**Images or examples** – 'aerial group photo around a birthday cake' *Example:*	**Sounds or rhythms** – words or phrases put together for impact – such as 'nearest and dearest', a sort of rhyme *Example:*

Use of English

Later in the unit you are going to write an advertisement for a photo app.

Adverbs to modify verbs and adjectives

Grammar presentation

We use adverbs to modify the meaning of verbs in a sentence. Adverbs are also used to modify or intensify the meaning of adjectives. Many advertisements use verbs and adverbs to encourage people to act.

1 Look at the sentences from the advertisement on pages 20–21. Underline the adverbs and explain how they modify the meaning of the verb or adjective.

  a …to tell the world your story, *exactly* as you want to tell it.

  b Achieve quirky, *previously* unseen angles of famous monuments…

  c Then post your snap *directly* on social media…

  d Take a panoramic shot when you've *successfully* scaled that mountain.

  e The first portable flying camera is *completely* safe to use inside.

2 Choose the best adverb for each sentence.

  a Post your beautiful creations *easily / effectively* on your favourite social media.

  b Add filters to your photos *effortlessly / incredibly*.

  c Your privacy is *totally / fully* guaranteed.

  d This *completely / quite* exclusive offer is only for a limited time.

  e Adjust the colours and brightness to achieve the results *definitely / exactly* the way you want.

3 Match the adverbs and adjectives to make common collocations.

  a highly   **i** unseen

  b absolutely   **ii** beautiful

  c previously   **iii** available

  d vitally   **iv** effective

  e eagerly   **v** important

  f widely   **vi** anticipated

4 Complete the following advertisement with the adverbs in the box.

> simply   completely   easily
>
> incredibly   quickly   directly
>
> constantly   safely

USBOOST

USBOOST is a handy device that allows you to free up space on your mobile phone **(a)** _____ and **(b)** _____. If you're the type of person who is **(c)** _____ snapping things on your phone, it's **(d)** _____ easy to fill your phone's memory. **(e)** _____ plug in USBoost and save all your photos and videos **(f)** _____. Then you can **(g)** _____ delete the photos and videos to leave your phone's memory **(h)** _____ free for more of your creations.

Vocabulary: advertising adjectives

Vocabulary presentation

Advertising uses positive adjectives that promote a product's virtues. But advertisements also use adjectives to provide potential customers with essential information.

5 Here are three sentences from the advertisement on pages 20–21. Copy the sentences and circle the adjectives that might appeal to readers of the advertisement.

a It's about giving you the most unique, flying camera technology to tell the world your story.

b Discover breathtaking heights where the only limit is your imagination.

c Snap unforgettable moments with your friends and family.

Find more adjectives in the advertisement that are used to appeal to the reader.

6 Which adjectives in this sentence provide information about the product?

The first portable flying camera is completely safe to use inside.

7 Copy the words in the box. Circle the adjectives that appeal and underline those that inform. Compare your answers with your partner.

useful	valuable	free
revolutionary	light	luxurious
attractive	simple	natural
strong	stylish	powerful

Tip

Read examples of advertising copy and product descriptions and focus on the adjectives that are used.

Cohesion: headings

Cohesion presentation

Headings can help you to organise your text and they help the reader to understand the structure and organisation of the writing.

8 Look back at the advertisement on pages 20–21. Why does the author use these headings and subheadings? What are the paragraphs about?

NEAREST AND DEAREST

INNOVATE YOUR WORKING LIFE

9 Complete the tips for writing headings using the words in the box.

key	benefits	short
	imperatives	visible

Five tips for writing great headings

a Keep them _____: use no more than seven or eight words.

b Make them _____: use bold letters and capitals or a larger font size.

c Use _____ words: your heading is like a signpost of what will come in the paragraph.

d Use _____: tell your readers what to do.

e Highlight the _____: always use positive words.

Guided writing

You have been asked to write an advertisement for a mobile phone app for editing photos. The app has all the usual features of a photo-editing app (filters, adjust colours and brightness, crop and rotate, etc.) but this app also has a special tool for making collages – making one image out of several different photos, all with different sizes and shapes.

The advertisement will appear on app stores where users can download the app.

Write the advertisement for the mobile app to go on app stores.

1 Work in pairs. Generate ideas for your advertisement. Write a list of features that photo-editing apps usually have and a short explanation of what each feature does. Here are some ideas:

- Filters: transform your original photo into something new – black and white, vintage, or different colour tones.

- Crop: change the shape and cut parts out to focus on the details.

- Rotate: straighten or turn your photo to the desired angle.

Tip

Use the internet to research different features of photo-editing apps.

2 Now decide which features you want to include in your promotional text.

- Remember to include the one(s) that make the product stand out from the competition.

- Note down ideas for how you will explain the features – use key words.

- Plan the structure of the information.

- Think of examples of how the features might be used to help the reader understand them.

- Think of different areas of life where the product could be useful: family photos, friends, holidays, work, etc.

Useful language

Phrases: *X is about more than…, It's about…, You won't believe…, It's easy to use and…, This amazing app has a full set of…, Unlike other apps,…, This app comes with…, Whether you want to…or …, this app will…, X has a wide range of…*

Adverbs: *exactly, directly, successfully, completely/totally, easily, effectively, effortlessly, highly, absolutely, simply, quickly*

Adjectives: *unique, breathtaking, unforgettable, stunning, useful, valuable, revolutionary, luxurious, attractive, simple, stylish, powerful, free, light, natural, strong*

Write: features

Write a short paragraph about the features you have chosen to describe.

a Use imperatives to address the reader directly.

b Use positive, convincing language to promote the benefits of the features.

c Use adverbs and adjectives to enhance your description.

d Explain what the features do and give examples of how they might be used.

e With your examples, suggest a lifestyle that you think would be attractive for your readers (family, friends, work, celebrations, etc.).

Write: introduction

When you have written the main body with the different features, write an introduction.

a The introduction should be a more general lead-in to the app.

b Include the name of the product and say what it does.

c Explain what the user can achieve with the app and how it will help them in a general way.

Write: headings

Now write the headings and subheadings for each paragraph, and a headline.

a Read the paragraphs and note down key words.

b Think of synonyms or related words.

c Try to think of interesting combinations for words.

d Use positive adjectives and adverbs.

e Keep your headings short (no more than eight words).

Here are some ideas for patterns:

- Imperative + noun: *Share life*
- Adverb + adjective: *Incredibly simple*
- Groups of three: *Choose, tap, save*
- A short sentence: *You'll love it.*

Write: logo, slogan, image

Finally, think of a logo for your product. Design a logo, come up with a slogan and find an image to accompany the promotional text.

Things to remember when writing an advertisement

- Promote your product or service.

- Write persuasively using a variety of structures.

- Structure the text around the benefits of your product.

- Capture the reader's attention through imperatives, headings, positive language.

- Use examples to suggest a lifestyle that will attract the reader.

- Write attractive headings and subheadings.

- Think of a logo, slogan and image to go with your product.

Check your first draft

When you have finished writing, be your own editor.

a Design your promotional text as a leaflet on a sheet of paper and proofread the copy.

b Share the leaflet with a partner or in a group and discuss how it could be improved in terms of both design and language.

Peer assessment

Check your partner's work for words or phrases that are repeated. Discuss alternatives that could be used instead.

Now write a second draft of your promotional text.

Independent writing

Write a promotional text or advertisement of 300–350 words.

Choose *one* of these ideas for a product or use your own.

- A paper diary/planner
- An app for students at your school
- A device for your cables and headphones

Write at least five paragraphs.

Follow these stages.

Stage 1 Generate ideas. Think of different features of the product that you want to highlight.

Stage 2 Put your ideas into a table. Include a slogan, headings, subheadings and key words.

- Which four or five features do you want to include?
- What order will you put them in?
- How will you introduce your product?

Stage 3 Write your advertisement in paragraphs. Use the checklist to make sure your advertisement is persuasive.

Writer's checklist: advertisements

- Have you promoted the main benefits of your product?
- Have you captured the reader's attention?
- Have you used a variety of adverbs and positive adjectives?
- Have you used headings and subheadings for each section?
- Have you come up with a good name, a slogan, a logo and an image?

Editor's checklist

Check

- that your ideas are organised into paragraphs
- your spelling and use of capital letters
- punctuation
- the grammar is correct – adverbs.

Final draft

When you have finished writing your advertisement, post it on the wall in your classroom.

Check your progress

I can:	Needs more work	Almost there	All done!
make planning choices with a clear sense of the task, purpose and audience			
demonstrate control of a variety of sentence structures for my intended purpose, to create the desired effect			
promote the benefits of a product or service for a reader			
write effective headings and subheadings to draw the reader's attention.			

3 Natural encounters

Your writing aim for this unit: To shape language to evoke a real-life situation

Writing objectives for first language English

In this unit, you will:

- shape and affect the reader's response by selecting from a wide and varied vocabulary

- use punctuation and grammatical choices to create a wide range of effects.

Writing and Use of English objectives for second language English

In this unit, you will:

- use different types of question

- learn the difference between *as* and *like*

- use correct punctuation – commas and dashes.

Key terms that you will learn: description essence 'if clause'

How can I describe a single object, person or animal in a convincing way?

How would you describe the image on the opening page of this chapter? You could say 'It's a bird with two wings flying across the sky'. But would that really capture how the bird looks? For a start, such a description lacks detail. What about the white tail feathers or the curved yellow beak? Or the fan-like tail? Or the way the eagle seems to soar effortlessly? Describing someone or something is about capturing his or her **essence**, and there are lots of ways to do it.

> ## Key terms
>
> **description**: something that tells you what someone or something is like
>
> **essence**: central idea or truth

Effective description

A good, close description of a person, animal or process should:

- focus on *specific features* of the thing/person/process described

- use some or all of the *senses* to give the reader a vivid picture

- use *vocabulary* that is *precise* and, in some cases, *related to the topic* or *process* (i.e. 'claw', 'beak', 'lift', 'grip', etc.)

- usually convey the *overall perspective* or *viewpoint* of the writer or narrator

- *capture the essence* of the person, thing, or experience.

Reading

The following extract is taken from a piece of travel writing in which the narrator is walking on a beach he hasn't visited before. Suddenly he thinks he spots a creature not usually seen on the shores of the United Kingdom. At first he thinks he is mistaken.

A Surprise Find

But the closer I get to the thing, the more it refuses to resolve itself into anything else. The closer I get, the more I know the thing is *exactly* what I think it is. It flips itself into the air again as I get closer and then I'm standing over it and there's no doubt left at all…

It's a shark.

It has the full complement of stiff, triangular fins, a long, curved tail, a big, round shark eye looking up at me from the sand, and a C-shaped mouth full of teeth.

It's a small, grey-brown, perfectly formed shark.

In length, it's about the same as the distance from my fingertips to my elbow, or perhaps a bit longer. Something between a foot-and-a-half and two feet, I guess. It must've been trapped as the tide retreated over the rock pools, then left high and dry when the sea pulled back altogether.

The shark springs again, then falls back to the sand.

Of course, if the shark doesn't go back into the water, it's going to die.

And at this moment, I realise it's incredibly important to me that the shark does not die. Not because I hate to see any animal suffer, but because there is a task to be performed here, and the task is so stripped down and obvious, and the situation so very **surreal**, that it takes on the unnatural, stylised air of myth or **parable**, despite the fact that it is also real and happening in the here-and-now. It's one of the strangest sensations of my entire life, but the facts seem perfectly clear.

I'm wet and cold and alone on a beach near Bognor Regis with a dying shark, and somehow I have to get this shark into the water.

I look up and down the beach.

There's nobody at all around.

Just me and the shark.

There's also nothing around that I can use to move the shark. The part of my brain that understands stories tells me this, tells me that's how it's going to be before I even begin to look, and sure enough, it's true. I try anyway. I try with all there is – a hopelessly small piece of driftwood and seaweed as a sort of scoop, but it's never going to work.

If I want to save the shark's life, the only way to do so is to reach down, grab hold of the shark around its middle, pick it up, and physically put it back in the sea myself.

1 As you read the text, think about these questions:

   a In what way is this account as much about the narrator's feelings as it is about the creature he discovers?

   b How does the way he has written the text make the process tense and exciting as well as descriptive?

And, to my surprise, I realise this is exactly what I'm about to do.

I push my jacket sleeve up my arm and look down at the shark, full of a sort of wild, giddy disbelief.

How to do this?

The shark has teeth, so I know I'm going to need to take hold of it quickly and firmly. But how solid are sharks? How robust? I have no idea. If I grab it too hard, am I going to kill it? On the other hand, if I don't grab it firmly enough, am I risking being bitten? Looking at the thing – very probably.

I decide I'm going to lunge and grab hold of it quickly and tightly behind the dorsal fin. If it turns out that sharks are actually fragile creatures – well.

I make a grab for the shark and know at once I've made the right choice – the creature is all rough skin and solid muscle, a gymnast's **bicep** wrapped in medium-grain sandpaper. The moment I have hold of it, the shark arches itself into a tense C-shape, like a taut bow, trying to get its mouth around to bite me. It doesn't wriggle or thrash at all, but tries with every bit of strength it has left to get its teeth to where my fingers are. But it can't.

I lift it up and take the few steps to the water's edge, shark held out in front of me, then I carefully lower it into the sea. I release my grip and pull my hand back fast.

The shark darts away amongst the submerged rock pools. In less than a second, it's gone.

I turn away, walk back up the beach.

It feels like something has been achieved, something great, something ridiculous, something not quite part of the real world – all of these things at once.

It's not until I get right back to the top of the beach that I realise I've made a mistake. I turn to look back at the place where I released the shark, and see a familiar black shape flipping and flopping on the sand.

The tide hasn't gone out. It's still *going* out.

All I'd managed to do was put the shark into another shallow, draining rock pool, so it could beach itself all over again. To save the shark's life, I'd have needed to actually wade out into the sea with it, past the rock pools, and let it go there.

I've underestimated the task. I've achieved nothing.

I set off back down the beach.

From 'You, Me and the Sea' by Steven Hall

How the text works

Do you remember what makes a good descriptive account? Here is how the writer makes it work. He:

- presents the situation to the reader as he experiences it, using the present tense for the most part ('I decide…')

- uses a variety of sentence and grammar forms to affect how we read the account (short sentences to express surprise, for example)

- uses precise vocabulary for the shark's appearance and how it moves ('dorsal fin')

- uses vivid imagery to convey a memorable picture of the shark ('a tense C-shape')

- uses questions to convey his inner thoughts as he tries to make sense of things.

Text analysis

It is important not to think of texts having only one purpose. If this text just described the appearance of a small shark found in the United Kingdom, it would be a simple description but probably not very interesting. After all, it is a small shark, not a huge killer! Equally, if it just told the story of the man finding the shark and trying to help it, without describing how it feels and moves, we would find it difficult to picture the scene in our mind. This text combines both purposes – to describe *and* to narrate.

1 This text works as a narrative as much as a description of a thing and a process because it raises questions throughout the text. Here is a timeline for the story. Copy and complete it, adding any questions the narrator has (some might be implied rather than stated directly).

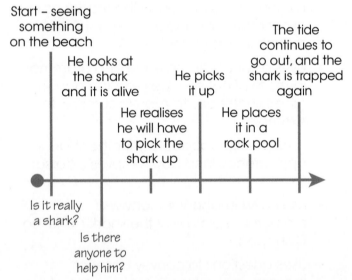

Reading closely

Being able to select particular information you are given in a text about one thing or person is a core skill in your English study, and it also links to how you might plan your own writing.

2 The key focus of this account is the shark itself. With a partner, go through the text and identify any information provided by the writer about the shark. You can copy and complete the diagram at the bottom of this page. Select the actual words or phrases from the text and you can even add drawings and diagrams.

3 Why is it important that the writer describes the shark in such detail? Discuss these possibilities with a partner or small group – there may be more than one reason.

   a Readers may not know what sharks look like

   b The writer is interested in wildlife and likes to keep a record of things he sees

   c Readers need to understand the situation he faced

   d He wants to frighten the reader

   e Some other reason.

4 The writer uses a number of techniques to convey his feelings about the situation.

   a One is to use simple sentences to express the reality of the situation. What three short simple sentences (one is a minor sentence) does he use to stress that there is no one to help him?

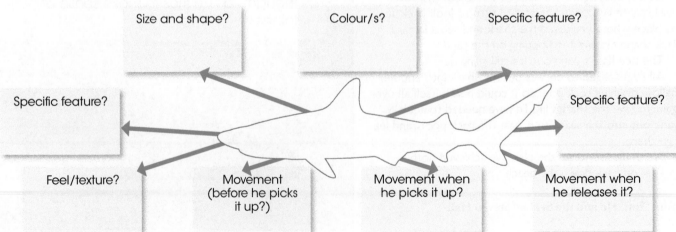

b He also uses a number of sentences with 'if clauses' to explain the consequences of doing (or not doing) something. Can you identify at least three sentences that use 'if clauses'?

c In each case:

   i What is the action being considered?

   ii What is the possible outcome? Is it certain, uncertain or probable?

d A third technique is to describe the situation as out of the ordinary or special in some way.

Can you match the following words or phrases to their meanings? You may need to find them in the text and read the full sentence or paragraph.

   i strangest sensations   laughable or idiotic

   ii giddy disbelief   weirdest feelings

   iii something ridiculous   dizzy with surprise

> ### Key term
>
> **'if clause'**: a part of a sentence that expresses a condition ('*If I run*, I might/could catch the bus' – it is possible I will but not certain)

5 You have already identified the various ways in which the shark is described. One of these is that the shark is 'taut like a bow' when the man picks it up. Write a sentence explaining what this suggests about how the shark feels in his hands.

It suggests the shark's body is…

Thinking about the text

6 Think carefully and then answer these questions.

a What does the phrase 'perfectly formed' tell us about how the man thinks about the shark?

b Why do you think he spends time deciding what to do?

c How would you describe the character of the man in the story? Consider these adjectives and decide which you think are most accurate.

foolish	nervous	decisive
frightened	thoughtful	thoughtless

d At the end of the text, it states he'd 'underestimated' the task. In what way?

React to the text

7 Work in pairs. Discuss these questions.

a In the extract, the man comes across a living creature that is trapped and will die if he doesn't help it. Have you ever been in, or known of anyone who has faced, a similar situation? When? What happened?

b Why do you think the man doesn't just leave the beach?

c How would you feel if you were in the same situation?

d In what way do you think the extract is effective in describing the encounter between the man and the shark? Think about:

- how clear a picture you get of the shark

- how well he describes the process of trying to save the shark

- how easy it is to understand the man's thoughts.

Use of English

Later in the unit you are going to write about an encounter with an animal.

Questions

Grammar presentation

Writers can express the inner thoughts of the narrator of a story. An effective way to convey doubts in the mind of the narrator is to use questions.

1 Match the questions used in the extract on pages 30–31 with the type.

a	How to do this?	**i**	*how* + adjective
b	But how solid are sharks?	**ii**	conditional question
c	If I grab it too hard, am I going to kill it?	**iii**	infinitive question

2 Complete the questions with the correct adjective after *How*.

a How _____ can a fish survive out of the water?

b How _____ is a sheep? Could I lift one up?

c How _____ is an elephant's skin?

d How _____ is this bridge? Will it support our weight?

e How _____ can a lizard run?

3 Match up the parts of each conditional question.

a	If I try to pick up a lizard,	**i**	am I going to damage its wings?
b	If I grab this bird,	**ii**	would you take it home?
c	If I get any closer to this bull,	**iii**	will it try to bite me?
d	If you found a stray cat,	**iv**	is it going to charge at me?

4 Complete the conditional questions with your own ideas.

a If I try to pick up the cat,

b If the dog starts to growl,

c If you owned a horse,

d If I see a bear,

5 Put the words in the correct order to make infinitive questions*.

a to / parents / tell / my / What / ?

b to / ask / Where / help / for / ?

c get / How / before / to / home / go / long / we / ?

d to / animal / help / this / How / ?

*Note that infinitive questions like these are not very common in English but the structure is more likely to appear in sentences: *I'm not sure what to tell my parents.*

Vocabulary: *as* and *like*

We use *as* and *like* in comparisons, but it's important to understand the difference and how they're used.

6 Look at the following examples from the extract on pages 30–31. How are the words *as* and *like* used?

a ...the shark arches itself into a tense C-shape, *like* a taut bow...

b It feels *like* something has been achieved...

c In length, it's about the same *as* the distance from my fingertips to my elbow...

d I try with all there is – a hopelessly small piece of driftwood and seaweed *as* a sort of scoop...

As is also a conjunction:

*It must've been trapped **as** the tide retreated.*

7 Choose the correct option to complete each sentence.

a He has dark, piercing eyes, *as / like* a hawk.

b I pick up a stick to use *as / like* a lever.

c I had never seen anything *as / like* this before.

d Picking up a dangerous animal is not *as / like* picking up a child.

e It's not the same *as / like* a snake but it moves *as / like* one.

f The creature was *as / like* long *as / like* my arm.

Certain pairs of words (*as* and *like*) can be confusing in English. As well as focusing on patterns in vocabulary, you have to pay attention to the ways in which certain individual words are used.

Punctuation: commas and dashes

We use both commas and dashes to separate words, groups of words or clauses in a sentence. Dashes are used when we want to highlight or draw attention to something. Look at these sentences from the extract on pages 30–31:

Looking at the thing – very probably.

If it turns out that sharks are actually fragile creatures – well.

The author wants to draw attention to the real possibility of being bitten in the first sentence. What is his intention in the second sentence?

8 Replace the commas with dashes in three of these sentences.

a There was only one thing I could do, put my hands out and grab the creature.

b I walked through the woods, turned off down a path, and went home.

c And suddenly I saw what the problem was, the animal was caught in barbed wire.

d As I got closer, I saw clearly, the head of a donkey reaching out of the water.

Guided writing

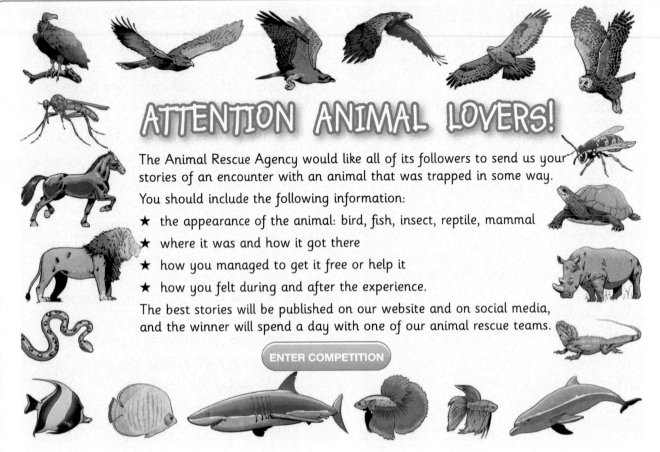

ATTENTION ANIMAL LOVERS!

The Animal Rescue Agency would like all of its followers to send us your stories of an encounter with an animal that was trapped in some way.

You should include the following information:

★ the appearance of the animal: bird, fish, insect, reptile, mammal

★ where it was and how it got there

★ how you managed to get it free or help it

★ how you felt during and after the experience.

The best stories will be published on our website and on social media, and the winner will spend a day with one of our animal rescue teams.

ENTER COMPETITION

Write your story about an encounter with an animal for the competition.

Think/Plan

1 Work in pairs. Generate ideas for your story. Here are some ideas to help you:

- You're in the country and you come across a donkey stuck knee-deep in mud.
- On a hike, you pass a field where you see a lamb caught in a wire fence.
- You come home to find a small bird (for example, a sparrow) flying around the kitchen.

2 Answer the following questions.

 a Where are you? What are you doing?

 b What animal do you see? What situation is the animal in?

 c What do you do to try to help it?

 d How do you feel?

3 Now organise the parts of your story. Think about what doubts and questions you might have as events unfold.

Tip

You could use the timeline on page 32 to help you plan your story.

Useful language

Phrases: *The closer I get, the more…, It must've been trapped…, And at this moment, I realise…, Somehow I have to…, To my surprise…, I decide I'm going to…, It feels like…, It's not until I… that…*

Questions: *How strong…?, How long…?, How solid…?, How heavy…?, How to get it out?, What to do?, If I…, will I/am I…?*

Comparisons: *It feels like/as if…, It looks like/as if…, It sounds like/as if…, I use [a stick] as [a lever], but…, (not) as…as, the same as*

Write: the encounter

Write the first part of your story.

a First, say where you are and what you are doing. Write in the present tense to give your story more immediacy.

b Describe your first encounter with the animal and your first impressions.

- *It looks like…*
- *It sounds like…*
- *The closer I get, the more…*

c Describe the animal.

- *It is…/It has…*
- *Like a…, it…*

Write: the rescue

Write about your attempts to rescue or liberate the animal.

a Describe your initial feelings and fears.

b Use questions to convey your feelings and doubts about what you are faced with.

c Say how you get over any fears or doubts you have.

Finish the story

Now write the end of your story.

In the story on pages 30–31, the writer realises his rescue wasn't entirely successful. End your story with the same idea: a first attempt gone wrong.

Things to remember when writing about a real-life situation

- Use some or all of the senses to give a vivid picture.
- Use present tenses to describe the situation as you see it.
- Use precise vocabulary to describe objects/people/animals/process.
- Convey the perspective and viewpoint of the narrator (you).
- Use vivid imagery to communicate memorable images.
- Use different types of sentence to express your inner thoughts.

Check your first draft

When you have finished writing your story, share it with your partner.

a First, describe your experience to your partner, saying what happened, how you felt, what you did, etc.

b Then give your partner your story to read.

c Discuss whether you have captured the vivid memories and viewpoint of the narrator in the written version by comparing it with the spoken version.

d Discuss ways to improve the written version.

Peer assessment

Make sure your partner's story is believable. After you've read it, discuss details and ask questions to clarify things you didn't understand.

Now write a second draft of the story.

Independent writing

Write a real-life encounter with a person, animal or object of 300–350 words.

Choose one of these ideas or use your own.

- Something shiny caught my eye and the closer I got, the more it glittered.
- It sounded like a baby crying at first…
- The old woman looked lost and a bit scared, standing still by a lamppost.

Follow these stages.

Stage 1 Generate ideas. Think about the situation you find yourself in; the object/animal/person; your actions; your feelings.

Stage 2 Put your ideas into a plan, using a timeline or table with the events and questions you ask yourself.

- Where will the story take place?
- What does the object/animal/person look like?
- What does the 'rescue' involve?
- How does it all end?

Stage 3 Write your story in paragraphs with a variety of structures, following your plan. Use the checklist to make sure your story evokes a real-life situation.

Writer's checklist: real-life encounters

- Have you described the object/animal/person, focusing on specific features?
- Have you used some or all of the senses to give your reader a vivid picture?
- Have you used precise vocabulary to describe situations and actions?
- Have you used a variety of sentence structures, including questions to convey your inner thoughts?
- Have you used dashes to highlight words and phrases?

Editor's checklist

Check

- that your ideas are organised into paragraphs
- your spelling and use of capital letters
- punctuation, especially commas and dashes
- the grammar is correct – questions.

Final draft

Once you have finished your description of a real-life encounter, post it on your blog or on the class website.

Check your progress

I can:	Needs more work	Almost there	All done!
describe a single object, animal or person			
use a range of punctuation and grammatical structures to aid cohesion, emphasise meaning and create a wide range of effects			
shape the reader's response through conscious choices from a wide variety of vocabulary			
convey feelings and vivid imagery to present a memorable picture.			

4 Listen up

Your writing aim for this unit: To write an effective review that is suitable for a particular audience

Writing objectives for first language English	**Writing and Use of English objectives for second language English**
In this unit, you will:	In this unit, you will:
• shape and affect the reader's response by selecting from a wide and varied vocabulary for a range of tasks, purposes and readers	• use the present simple and present perfect simple active and passive forms
• write to analyse, review and comment	• learn words and phrases related to music
• demonstrate control of a wide variety of sentence types.	• use correct style – song and album titles.

Key terms that you will learn: style audience genre

How can I use language to review in an informative but entertaining way?

How do you decide if a television programme or film is worth watching? How do you decide if a particular video game is worth playing, or whether a piece of music is worth downloading or buying? Make a note of the people who influence you – and also *what* you want to find out.

If you have been following this course, you will already have encountered reviews – but reviews vary according to what is being reviewed and the audience that will read them.

Effective entertaining reviews

An entertaining review should:

- be *relevant* – about a topic, event or product that is available at the time of writing

- *match* its **style** and language to its **audience** (who will read or see it)

- *show knowledge* of the topic or thing being reviewed

- *interest* the *reader* – whether that is through giving a *strong viewpoint* or an *entertaining* view of the product.

Key terms

style: the way something is done or written

audience: the people or type of people who watch a film or television programme

genre: a type of writing or art with a particular style

Reading

The following review is of an **album** release by a popular band.

1 As you read the text, think about these questions:

  a How does the writer show knowledge of the band and their music?

  b How strong are his or her views about this album?

BTS album *Love Yourself: Answer* review

Suga, J-Hope and Rap Monster solos, Korean drums. BTS Army are gonna love this.

K-pop rappers show their chops *on solo* tracks, *band sends a message to Korean youth about self-love, and* single *Idol sees them* don *traditional* garb *and blend pop with ancient percussion, on an album that* cements *BTS place as kings of the* **genre**.

With the release of the *Love Yourself: Answer* album on Friday, K-pop giants BTS have closed a momentous chapter in their record-breaking career that has seen them become the biggest Korean act internationally. The final release of the two-and-a-half-year-long *Love Yourself* album series, only seven of its 25 tracks are new, with the rest drawn from previous albums in the series. Despite being a largely repackaged album, it will satisfy diehard fans and pique the interest of those who are new to the group. In particular, the boy band's fans (known as the BTS Army) will be excited to hear solo tracks by band members who usually rap – Rap Monster, Suga and J-Hope.

J-Hope's 'Trivia: Just Dance' is a fun **bubblegum** dance track about the excitement felt in the early stages of a romance. His line, "Even when I'm in the practice room/I'm happy because I'm with you" could be a nod to the huge number of fans worldwide watching BTS's every move. 'Trivia: Love' showcases Rap Monster's talents as vocalist as he skilfully pulls off an R&B love song. He employs some clever puns in Korean in his lyrics, although overseas fans will have to work these out for themselves.

Suga, who has often proven his skill at writing melancholy lyrics, does it again in 'Trivia: Seesaw', a fizzy, synthesiser-driven number that charts the end of a relationship. The vocalist laments he is now "alone on the see-saw" as the track draws to a close. 'Epiphany', one of the album's stand-out tracks, is a thought-provoking ballad. Sounding deceptively like a love song, it is actually about the importance of loving oneself – a message that hopefully will resonate in South Korea.

The new single 'Idol', on which band members are joined by an international star, is an intriguing mix of tribal dance beats and traditional Korean rhythms. BTS members grunt out centuries-old Korean 'response words' (usually heard at traditional folk music performances to express the audience's approval) in between singing about the woes of being international stars.

In the accompanying video, BTS don traditional Korean garb, and the track itself features ancient Korean percussion instruments such as the *ggwenggari*, *jing* and *janggu*. Although this is not the first track to combine traditional Korean music with modern grooves – artist Seo Taeji did it in the early 1990s – BTS have taken it to the next level by bringing in an international star and exposing Korean traditions to a huge global audience.

Although padded with plenty of previously released material, such as the earlier hits 'Fake Love' and 'The Truth Untold' (featuring US DJ Steve Aoki), the new album should ensure BTS's reign as the kings of K-pop will continue.

Nemo Kim from *South China Morning Post* website (www.scmp.com)

Key language features

present tenses

music-related vocabulary

song and album titles

Glossary

album: a collection of recorded songs

chops: skills

single: single track of music (one song)

don: put on

garb: clothing

pique: to arouse interest

bubblegum: appealing to teenagers

R&B: contemporary form of rhythm and blues, often featuring hip-hop or rap

see-saw: two-seated children's playground object that tilts up and down

woes: sorrows or worries

padded: filled out with or stuffed

How the text works

Do you remember what makes a good review? Here is how the writer makes it work. He/she:

- uses present tenses ('*show* their chops') to indicate this is a new recording, and other tenses to talk about background or how the music will be received

- uses vocabulary that will interest an audience that follows music ('bubblegum')

- uses vocabulary that shows knowledge of music and recording ('lyrics', 'ballad', etc.)

- expresses opinion through language choices, such as verbs and adjectives ('*clever* puns', '*cements* BTS' place').

Text analysis

1 As a way of getting into the text, work with a partner and imagine you are presenting a music review show on television or online.

First, divide up the text, deciding who will read each part. If you have a copy of the review you could mark it up, highlighting your sections. If you want to be really clever, you could add in questions or prompts. For example, 'So, Jay, what are the stand-out tracks?'

Then, read/perform the text as if in front of a camera or live studio audience. One of you could start: *'Welcome to Music Review Weekly. Today we are talking about the new BTS album – Love Yourself: Answer'*.

Depending on whether you think the review is positive or negative, adapt your tone to suit your viewpoint, perhaps emphasising particular words.

2 Now, on your own, reread the text, and think about how it has been structured. Does it have:

a a title for the review?

b a summary section, which is rather like the conclusion in giving a broad idea of the music and the reviewer's thoughts?

c an introduction that gives some background to the release of the album?

d body paragraphs that provide specific details about the music and the tracks?

e any additional paragraphs providing related or connected information?

f a concluding paragraph that sums up the reviewer's views?

Reading closely

3 Use **a–f** from Activity 2 as labels: copy them out and place them against the relevant sections of the review. This should give you a sense of how it is organised.

Now, consider what *specific* details each section provides.

a In the summary section, beginning 'K-pop rappers show their chops…', the reviewer mentions three things worth noting. The first is that the rappers in the band each have their own songs. What other two things about the album does he/she mention?

b What four tracks from the album are mentioned in the second and third paragraphs?

c In the fourth paragraph, the reviewer mentions three traditional elements that appear on *Idol*. What are they?

d How does the fifth paragraph also comment on the 'traditional' elements of the music? Complete this sentence explaining your thoughts:

The fifth paragraph contains references to _____ *and also* _____.

e The final paragraph does two things: it sums up what the reviewer thinks but also looks forward to the future for BTS. What clause in the sentence tells us that BTS are likely to continue to succeed?

4 The writer's word choices show he/she knows a lot about music and bands, and how to sum up how good they are.

a In the second paragraph, there are a number of music-related references. Identify nouns that mean:

i singer

ii a follower or supporter of a band

iii song from an album

iv the words from a song.

b In the third paragraph, he/she uses several words or phrases to describe the music. Check the context in the sentence and then write down what you think each word or phrase means. (Sometimes evidence is provided by the rest of the sentence.)

i melancholy

ii fizzy

iii laments

iv thought-provoking

v deceptively

c We get a strong sense of how popular BTS are. Identify any words or phrases that mean:

i sales of their records are higher than anyone else's (first paragraph)

ii the type of fans who will like anything they do (first paragraph)

iii BTS are like all-powerful rulers of a country (last paragraph).

Thinking about the text

5 Think carefully and then answer these questions.

a Do you think the writer is an *actual* fan of the band – or just someone who appreciates their success? Why do you think this?

b How successful are BTS? Based on the review (not your own knowledge!) what evidence (if any) is there that they are successful around the world?

c Which of these statements do you think best describes BTS's music, based on the review?

i fun, frothy and forgettable

ii slow, sad and serious

iii varied, but full of emotions

iv weird, wacky and mad

React to the text

6 Work in pairs. Discuss these questions.

a Do you think modern bands like BTS should mix modern music and traditional music? Why/why not?

b Are you a fan of any one singer or band? What makes you like them?

c In what ways is this an effective review of BTS's album? Think about:

- whether you learn enough about the album and its tracks

- whether the reviewer gives you his or her view about the album

- whether it is written in a style you find engaging and interesting.

Use of English

Later in the unit you are going to write a music review.

Present tenses: simple and perfect

Grammar presentation

In reviews, writers use present tenses. The present perfect is used to give some background and the present simple is used to comment on the work under review.

1 Look at the following sentences and phrases from the review on pages 40–41. Identify the tense in each one.

   a K-pop giants BTS *have closed* a momentous chapter in their record-breaking career that *has seen* them become the biggest Korean act internationally.

   b *Trivia: Love showcases* Rap Monster's talents as vocalist as he skilfully *pulls off* an R&B love song.

   c …band members *are joined* by an international star,…

2 Answer these questions about the sentences in Activity 1.

   Which sentence or phrase…

   a gives background information?

   b presents something recent that connects the past and the present?

   c comments on something happening now or around this time?

3 Choose the correct form to complete each sentence.

   a The band, who *spend / have spent* the last year touring, *decide / have decided* to release a live album.

   b The multitalented vocalist Ken *sings / has sung* beautifully on *Shining Stars* but *leaves / has left* the lyrics writing to the guitarist Bunny, with mixed results.

   c The album *is filled / has been filled* with catchy pop clichés, which Wu *delivers / has delivered* with appropriate enthusiasm.

   d Sami *often demonstrates / has often demonstrated* her immense vocal talent and her new album *doesn't disappoint / hasn't disappointed*.

4 Complete this short review of a new single.

★★★★☆

Single: Runaway Girl

XT Rain (feat. Yoli G.)

XT Rain's career **(a)** _____ (see) her move between music styles several times over the years. Her new single, called *Runaway Girl*, **(b)** _____ (remind) us of the hip-hop style at the start of her career and **(c)** _____ (feature) a collaboration with Yoli G. from Spain. The song **(d)** _____ (start) with a children's choir and then **(e)** _____ (take) off with an excellent piano part. XT Rain and Yoli G. **(f)** _____ (interact) skilfully in the chorus, which **(g)** _____ (create) a wonderful effect. This new song **(h)** _____ (take) a long time to appear, but it certainly **(i)** _____ (stand) out from her previous material and we're sure her fans will be delighted.

Vocabulary: music

In a good music review, the writer has to show some knowledge of different aspects of the topic. These include genres, instruments, production and the music business.

5 Copy the table and complete it with one or two more words from the review on pages 40–41.

Production	beat
Band/ instruments	drums
Parts of an album	track
Genres	pop
Marketing	release

Add more words to the table from your own knowledge.

6 Here is a music quiz. Choose the correct answers, then compare your answers with your partner.

a What is a band with five members called?

 A a quintet

 B a five-piece band

 C both answers are correct

b The lead singer usually sings the:

 A solo

 B melody

 C chords

c ...and the backing singers usually sing:

 A notes

 B keys

 C harmonies

d What is the name of the type of song that will send you to sleep?

 A lullaby

 B chorus

 C anthem

e Which of these is not a musical genre?

 A jazz

 B rock

 C electric

 D indie

Classifying vocabulary can help you to remember words and phrases better because it helps you to organise them.

Punctuation: titles

Styles differ for the titles of albums and songs. In the review on pages 40–41, the album title goes in inverted commas and song titles in italics. All the words in the titles have capital letters.

7 Correct the mistakes in each sentence.

a Muha's new album called five fingers will be released next week.

b Their latest single the power in me is a mix of rock and heavy percussion.

c The album ends with a power ballad called on a bright day.

d The first track on think again is a riotous anthem called hot sand.

Guided writing

WE'RE LOOKING FOR REVIEWERS!

Do you have what it takes to work as a reviewer for Music Issues?

If you're interested in writing reviews for us of new releases, singles, albums, or concerts, send us an original review of a recently released album by a singer or band you like.

Make sure you do your research and, remember, you have to be honest!

Deadline: 6 March

Write a music review for the music magazine.

Research

1 Before you plan your review, you should do some research to find out as much as you can about the album. Work in pairs. Tell your partner what you found out.

a Where was it recorded?

b What is the background to the album? Was there any special reason for making it?

c Who wrote and performed each song?

d Are there any guest artists featured on the album?

e Who is the main audience for the album?

2 Listen to the album several times. As you listen, write notes on each track: your feelings, aspects of the music that catch your attention, lyrics that you like, stand-out tracks.

> **Tip**
>
> When you're writing a review (of an album, film, book, meal, product), it's best to jot down notes as you go along rather than leave them until the end.

3 Now plan how you are going to structure your review. Here is a possible structure for you to use.

- Title of album/name of band/number of stars out of five

- Summary paragraph: introduction – background – general overview

- Body paragraphs – individual tracks or elements of album (i.e. tracks featuring a particular singer or in a particular style)

- Conclusion – album's appeal/ audience – predictions for the album/ band/genre.

> **Useful language**
>
> **Phrases:** *With the release of…, it will satisfy diehard fans…, a fun bubblegum dance track about…, a fizzy, synthesiser-driven number which…, one of the album's stand-out tracks…, The new single…is an intriguing mix of…*
>
> **Adjectives:** *catchy, raucous, rich, upbeat, complex, fresh, funky, melodic, lush, rich*
>
> **Music words:** *track, single, album, number, drums, synthesiser, guitar, bass, vocals, beat, rhythm, groove, jam, pop, rap, R&B, rock, indie, funk, soul, line, lyrics, chorus, refrain*

Write: first paragraph

Write the first paragraph of your review.

Include the following information:

- the name of the band and the album
- the release date and the time since the band's last album
- the number of tracks
- potential audience/appeal.

You should also write a headline and a subtitle.

Write: main body

Write the main body of your review.

Describe some stand-out tracks or aspects of the album. Include information about the music, lyrics, style and content, and use interesting adjectives to describe these aspects. Write two or three paragraphs.

a Use the present perfect simple to explain the background to the track.

b Use the present simple to comment on the different aspects of the track.

c Show your knowledge of music: instruments, styles, production, etc.

Did you know?

Reviewers often pack a lot of information into the sentences in the main body. Look at this example from the review on pages 40–41.

Suga, who has often proven his skill at writing melancholy lyrics, does it again in *Trivia: Seesaw*, a fizzy, synthesiser-driven number that charts the end of a relationship.

style and content

background information

Write: conclusion

Now write the conclusion of your review.

Use the final paragraph to comment on the future of the band, album and/or genre. Here are some ideas to help you.

- *This album will surely consolidate...*
- *This new material will definitely appeal to...*
- *It may not be their best material so far, but it will...*
- *Perhaps this new album will help to put [band] on the international stage.*

Things to remember when writing a review

- Write about something relevant at the time of writing.
- Match the style and language to your audience.
- Demonstrate your knowledge of the topic through the vocabulary.
- Give a strong viewpoint in an entertaining way.
- Use the present perfect to explain the background.
- Use the present simple to comment on what you are reviewing.

Check your first draft

When you have finished writing your review, share it with your partner.

a Check that your partner has included all of the correct information.

b Pay attention to whether his/her opinions are clear and consistent.

c Assess whether the style and language are appropriate for the type of reader.

Peer assessment

Decide on a set of criteria for your partner to use to evaluate your work.

Now write a second draft of your review.

Independent writing

Write an entertaining and informative music review of 350–400 words.

Choose *one* of these for your review, or use your own.

- An album by an artist you have never heard before.

- The latest album by a band or artist from a genre you don't normally listen to.

- Invent a band and review their debut album.

Write four to five paragraphs.

Follow these stages.

Stage 1 Do your research. Listen to the album a few times and take notes. If you are inventing your own band, think of the name, band members' names, genre, album title and tracks.

Stage 2 Put your ideas into a plan, using a mind map. Note down ideas for the following:

- Basic information and star rating

- Introduction: general impressions

- Main body: stand-out tracks – background and comments

- Conclusion: summarise your opinions and make predictions about the band/album/genre.

Stage 3 Write your review in paragraphs, following your plan. Use the checklist to make sure your review is both informative and entertaining.

Writer's checklist: reviews

- Is the content of the review about a product that is available now?

- Have you written in a style that is appropriate for your audience?

- Have you demonstrated your knowledge of the topic through your use of vocabulary?

- Have you used a variety of present tenses to give background and comment on what is on the album?

- Have you given a strong viewpoint and expressed your opinion clearly?

- Have you written a headline, subheading and given a star rating?

Editor's checklist

Check

- that your ideas are organised into paragraphs

- your spelling and use of capital letters

- punctuation, especially in direct speech

- the grammar is correct – present tenses.

Final draft

Once you have finished your review, post it on an internet store or on the class website.

Check your progress

I can:	Needs more work	Almost there	All done!
write a review in an informative and entertaining way			
match the style of the review to my audience			
show my knowledge of the topic through my language choices			
use the correct style for album and track titles.			

5 Past reflections

Your writing aim for this unit: To write effective and interesting commentaries

Writing objectives for first language English	**Writing and Use of English objectives for second language English**
In this unit, you will:	In this unit, you will:
• write to analyse, review and comment	• use the passive and active past tense forms
• develop a range of registers and a personal voice	• learn words and phrases related to health and illness
• select the most appropriate text format, layout and presentation to create impact and engage the reader.	• use cohesion – time expressions.

Key terms that you will learn:　commentary　anecdote　time/sequence connectives

How do I comment on an aspect of everyday life in an interesting way?

What 'everyday things' give you pleasure? Some people enjoy cleaning their teeth, others ironing, others drinking a cup of coffee at 11 o'clock. Even tidying up a drawer can be satisfying! Talk about your everyday routine and which of the things you actively enjoy – and which you dislike. In what way do some things do you good? Are they relaxing? Refreshing?

Effective commentaries on life

A good **commentary** should:

- consider an *aspect of life* in a *balanced, thoughtful* way

- *explore* it in *new* or *original* ways that provoke *interest* from the reader

- often include *personal* **anecdotes** or *experiences*

- use a *mix* of *factual references* and *views* or *ideas*.

> ### Key terms
>
> **commentary**: a text that offers observations or reflections on aspects of life
>
> **anecdote**: a short personal tale or story, often funny

Reading

The following text by Chinese writer Adeline Yen Mah is autobiographical and deals with a very common aspect of life for many people all over the world – tea!

1 As you read the text, think about these questions:

   a The text is divided into halves: what does the writer focus on in each half?

   b What overall view do you think the writer has about tea?

Time for Tea

Next to water tea is the most popular drink in China. Tea (called chá 茶 in Chinese) was first cultivated during the Han **dynasty** (220–206 **BCE**) and became popular among the rich in the Tang dynasty (618–906 CE). From then on, the habit spread across the land. By the eighteenth century, the British had also acquired a taste for tea-drinking and were importing increasing amounts – up to 30 million pounds per year in the 1830s. In order to improve the balance of trade, Britain started exporting **opium** from India to China. Eventually, this opium trade led to the Opium War between China and Britain in 1842. By the 1880s, British tea imports had risen to 150 million pounds per year.

Recent scientific studies reveal that leaves from the common Chinese tea plant, *Camellia sinensis*, contain certain potent antioxidants known as **polyphenols**, which may help to prevent heart disease and cancer. There are three types of tea: green, oolong and black. Green tea is made by quickly steaming the freshly plucked green leaves; whereas both oolong and black teas are made by **fermenting** and air-drying the leaves (thereby causing oxidation, which causes the leaves to turn brown or black) and then crushing them. All three teas contain roughly equal amounts of protective chemicals, although their forms may differ.

A cup of tea contains approximately half as much caffeine as a cup of coffee. More importantly, its polyphenols prevent **DNA** and cell damage caused by **free radicals**. As **antioxidants**, these polyphenols are more potent than vitamins C or E. Tea appears to lower **serum cholesterol** and *triglycerides**, and protect against heart disease and stroke. In animal studies, polyphenols have been shown to ward against the development of rheumatoid arthritis and skin cancers, as well as cancers of the mouth and digestive tract. Further experiments are being carried out on humans.

My Aunt Baba was an **inveterate** tea drinker. She always kept a **thermos** of hot water and

a small jar of *long jing* 龍井茶 (dragon's well) green tea from Hang Zhou in our room. One of my earliest memories is that of my aunt waking me at the crack of dawn on the mornings when I was scheduled to sit for important tests. She would wipe my face with a hot, moist towel and make me sit up in bed. Then she would hand me a fragrant cup of steaming green tea while she quizzed me on my homework.

As I sat sipping my tea, bleary-eyed and half-asleep, I would watch her flipping through the pages of my textbooks with a frown of concentration, hoping and dreading to trip me up at the same time. I did not know then that these were special moments which I would treasure for the rest of my life. I longed to snuggle back under the quilt but dared not even protest because I was well aware that my aunt hated getting up early and was only doing it for me.

Whenever I made a mistake in my answers, she would urge me to take another sip of tea, think hard and try again. 'Tea sharpens the mind, soothes the stomach and nourishes your qi! Remember this!'

Yes! I never forgot! Especially her unwavering belief in me and the feeling that I must never let her down. Even today, getting up at 5 a.m. to sit in front of my computer while reading a scientific paper stating that tea contains polyphenols which help prevent cancer and chronic heart disease, I see her eyes poring anxiously over my printouts. 'Don't worry! Don't worry!' I tell her, over and over. 'I won't disappoint you! One day, you'll be proud of me. I promise.'

*Triglycerides are breakdown products of fat and are harmful to the body.

From *Watching the Tree* by Adeline Yen Mah

Glossary

dynasty: one family's long rule

BCE: Before Common Era

opium: a strong drug made from poppy seeds

polyphenols: nutrients found in plants

fermenting: conversion of carbohydrates to acid or alcohol

DNA: deoxyribonucleic acid – the individual genetic 'make-up' of people

free radical: a type of atom

antioxidant: substance that might prevent cell damage

serum cholesterol: your blood cholesterol

inveterate: deep-rooted

thermos: vessel for keeping liquids hot

quilt: thick bedcover

qi: Chinese concept of internal energy or life force

How the text works

Do you remember what makes a good commentary? Here is how the writer makes it work. She:

- uses a *range of tenses*, appropriate to the *specific purpose* of each section

- includes *factual information* that fills in the background for the topic

- suggests *her own view* through the *language choices* ('may help to prevent') rather than stating them explicitly

- uses *personal references*, linking the consumption of tea to her beloved aunt.

Text analysis

1 Although this text is a 'commentary', it in fact has lots of purposes. Which of the following purposes can you find evidence for in the text? Discuss each one with a partner.

a Recounts the history of tea, in chronological order

b Persuades the reader that they must drink tea rather than coffee or anything else

c Describes the process for making certain teas

d Explains how tea became popular

e Reviews tea she has bought

f Comments on her life now and how it is connected with tea

g Explains the potential health benefits

h Describes Aunt Baba's love of tea

i Narrates an anecdote from her childhood with Aunt Baba.

Reading closely

2 Once you have decided which of the purposes above match the text, copy them out onto small pieces of paper and see if you can match them to the text by placing them over a specific section, as shown below.

Describes Aunt Baba's love of tea

> My Aunt Baba was an inveterate tea drinker. She always kept a thermos of hot water and a small jar of long jing 龍井茶 (dragon's well) green tea from Hang Zhou in our room.

3 In the first part of the text, the writer explains the facts and processes around tea. What does the reader find out?

a During which dynasty was tea first grown in China?

b How much tea did the British import in the 1830s?

c What might the antioxidants in tea prevent?

d How much caffeine does coffee have compared with tea (on average)?

e What other things does tea seem to protect against?

4 As stated earlier, the language used in each section of the text matches its purpose.

a In the first paragraph there are a number of **time/sequence connectives** to help explain the history of tea. ('...tea was *first* cultivated...') Can you identify three other connective words or phrases in the first paragraph?

b In the second paragraph, the benefits of tea are explored using a lot of 'process' verbs such as 'steaming'. What other two participle verbs also describe the process?

c Later, the writer's aunt says, 'Tea <u>sharpens</u> the mind, <u>soothes</u> the stomach and <u>nourishes</u> your qi.' What does each of the underlined verbs mean (in context)? Explain in your own words.

> **Key term**
>
> **time/sequence connectives**: words or phrases that indicate a specific time at which something happens, or the order of events: before noon, firstly, next, later, etc.

Thinking about the text

The text appears to be mostly about tea and its properties, but it is really much more than that.

5 Think carefully and then answer these questions.

a The writer states about her aunt's help:

> I did not know then that these were special moments which I would treasure for the rest of my life.

Discuss with a friend or small group what the writer means by this. Consider these options:

i She does not value those memories as they were only important to her aunt.

ii As a child she could not look into the future and judge how precious the time with her aunt was.

iii She does not know if the memories are special or not.

iv She knew as a child how precious her time with her aunt was.

v Something else?

b What impression does the writer give of her aunt? Try to support what you say with reference to the text. If you can, try to include a quotation from the text. This is a skill you will need more and more as your work progresses. Use this scaffold to help you:

The impression I get of Aunt Baba is of a _____ person who _____ _____ .

This can be seen when she _____ _____ .

React to the text

6 Work in pairs. Discuss these questions.

a In the extract, Aunt Baba insists on the author drinking tea to make her revise more effectively. What do you like to eat or drink to help you concentrate? Does it work?

b Why do you think the writer still wants to impress her aunt, even now she is an adult?

c How effective is the extract in exploring tea and commenting on its effects and properties? Think about:

- whether you have learned anything about tea you didn't know

- the ways in which the writer makes the text personal as well as informative.

Use of English

Later in the unit you are going to write about a food you like or enjoyed when you were younger.

Past tenses

Grammar presentation

In the text on pages 50–51, the writer gives a short history of tea and, later on, some personal memories from her life. In both parts, she uses a range of past tenses, both active and passive. Remember that we use the passive voice when we don't want to say who did the action, or when it's not important.

1 Identify the different past tenses in the following sentences from the text (pages 50–51). Then answer the questions.

   a Tea (called chá 茶 in Chinese) *was* first *cultivated* during the Han dynasty (220–206 BCE) and *became* popular among the rich in the Tang dynasty (618–906 CE).

   b By the eighteenth century, the British *had* also *acquired* a taste for tea-drinking and *were importing* increasing amounts.

   c Then she *would hand* me a fragrant cup of steaming green tea…

      i Which tense expresses an action in the past that happened before another past action?

      ii Which tense expresses a habitual action in the past?

      iii Which tense is used for an action that is continuous?

2 Choose the correct past tense forms to complete each sentence.

   a My aunt *had already had / was already having* two cups of tea when I *offered / was offered* to make a pot.

   b I *studied / was studying* for my maths exam when my mum *came / had come* in with a cup of hot chocolate.

   c Coffee *was introduced / was introducing* into India from Yemen in the sixteenth century.

   d Every day before school, my father *would tie / was tying* our ties and while we *had put / were putting* on our shoes, he *would pick up / was picking up* his briefcase and all our school bags in one hand.

3 Complete each sentence with the correct forms of the tenses in brackets.

   a By the time potatoes _____ (arrive) in Europe, the Incas _____ (grow) them for many thousands of years.

   b The ancient Wari civilisation _____ (spring) up around Lake Titicaca in South America around 500 CE, and _____ (expand) to a population of 500,000 thanks to the fact that they _____ (cultivate) potatoes.

   c It is said that potatoes _____ (introduce) into Ireland by the English explorer Sir Walter Raleigh.

   d When I _____ (grow) up in Ireland, my family _____ (eat) potatoes every day.

Vocabulary: health and illness

The commentary on pages 50–51 includes a section about the health benefits of tea.

4 Complete this extract from the text on pages 50–51 with the words in the box.

> skin cancers   heart disease
>
> arthritis   cholesterol   strokes

Tea appears to lower serum
(a) _____ and triglycerides,
and protect against **(b)** _____
and **(c)** _____. In animal
studies, polyphenols have been shown
to ward against the development of
rheumatoid **(d)** _____ and
(e) _____, as well as cancers of
the mouth and digestive tract.

5 Match each symptom to the correct remedy.

a a sprained ankle   **i** lotion
b a bruise   **ii** sleeping pills
c insomnia   **iii** painkillers and a bandage
d a rash   **iv** ice

6 Complete each sentence with the correct verb from the box.

> lower   prevent   suffer
>
> protect   relieve

a Regular exercise and a healthy diet
can _____ heart disease.

b These pills should _____ the
pain a bit.

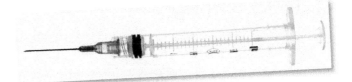

c This vaccination will _____ you
against the measles.

d Avoiding fatty foods will help to
_____ your cholesterol.

e People who _____ from
insomnia have trouble sleeping.

Organise your vocabulary by topic, and within each topic learn different aspects. For example, in health and illnesses, you should learn different illnesses, symptoms, remedies, verbs, phrases, etc.

Cohesion: time and sequence

When explaining the history of something, describing a process or narrating a personal memory, connectives are important to help the reader place an action in time or in order.

7 Choose the correct connective to complete each sentence.

a *After / Following* studying for many years, I *eventually / meanwhile* became a doctor.

b *By / At* the eighteenth century, China was exporting millions of tonnes of tea.

c *All the time / Whenever* we gave the wrong answer, our teacher would pretend to cry.

d *First / Firstly*, the tips of the leaves are cut off and they are *consequently / subsequently* dried.

Guided writing

ATTENTION!

The 'Dinnertime' food blog would like you, its valued readers, to share your commentaries on something you eat or drink regularly and that has a strong memory associated with it. Your commentary should include some historical information, health benefits or risks, and a personal anecdote associated with the food or drink in question.

Write a commentary for the food blog.

Think

1 Work in pairs. Generate ideas for your commentary. Answer the questions to help you.

   a What food do you like that has a special importance for you?

   b Do you know anything about its history: where it comes from, when it was first made, etc.?

   c What do you know about its health benefits or risks?

   d Do you have a specific memory or anecdote you associate with the food or drink? Tell your partner.

Tip

Most texts that you write require some research. Knowing exactly what you're looking for in key words will help you focus your research and save you time.

2 Do some research about the food or drink you have chosen. Use these ideas to help you. The words in brackets are ideas based on tea – the subject of the text on pages 50–51.

   a **popularity**: find out some data about where and how much it is sold and consumed (*tea consumption worldwide; tea sales figures*)

   b **origin**: where it comes from; where it was invented (*origin of tea; history of tea; where was tea invented*)

   c **how it came to your country**: (*tea consumption in [country]; history of tea in [country]*)

   d **how it's made**: (*how is tea made*)

   e **health benefits/risks**: (*health benefits of tea; health effects of tea; why is tea good/bad for you*)

Take notes as you research. Note down dates, figures and key words.

3 Plan your commentary. Use the following structure to help you. Organise your notes in a table like this:

Popularity/history	
How it's made	
Health benefits/risks	
Personal memory/ anecdote	

Useful language

Phrases: *[food/drink] is the most popular…, [food/drink] was first grown/ cultivated/manufactured in [country], …originally comes from…, …recent scientific studies reveal…, [food/drink] contains…*

Health/illness: *heart disease, insomnia, cancer, cholesterol, stroke, arthritis*

Health verbs: *prevent, lower, protect against, ward against, relieve, suffer from*

Write: background

Write the first few paragraphs of your commentary.

Follow these steps.

a First, write a short paragraph about the popularity and history of the food or drink you have chosen. Include dates, figures and comparisons with other food/drink.

b In the second paragraph, describe the process of how it is made/cultivated/manufactured. Use present tense passive structures.

c In the third paragraph, describe some of the health benefits or risks of your food/drink. Refer to research into the food/drink or some of its ingredients (for example, sugar, wheat, etc.).

Write: commentary

Now write the personal commentary on the food or drink you have chosen. This should be a personal memory or anecdote you associate with the food or drink.

Use these ideas to help you.

a What is your earliest memory of the food/drink?

b Is there a particular person you associate with it?

c When did you eat/drink it? What were you doing?

d Did you enjoy the experience? Why?/Why not?

e Why do you still remember it? How is it relevant to your life now?

Check your first draft

When you have finished writing, be your own editor.

- Read your commentary again and compare it to the extract on pages 50–51. Have you followed the same structure?

- Check that your commentary is coherent – that the different parts of the text work well together.

- Think of ways you can improve the coherence.

Now write a second draft of your commentary.

Independent writing

Write a commentary of 350–400 words.

Choose *one* of these ideas or use your own.

- A task or chore that you do at home.
- A means of transport that you use regularly.
- A shop you go to frequently.

Write at least four or five paragraphs.

Follow these stages.

Stage 1 Generate ideas. Think back to those 'everyday things' that give you pleasure that you talked about in the task on page 50. Do some background research about the activity – history, popularity, effects on your health.

Stage 2 Put your ideas into a plan, using a table. The table can be divided into the following sections:

- popularity, background, history
- process
- health effects
- personal memory/anecdote.

Stage 3 Write your commentary in paragraphs, following your plan. Use the checklist to make sure your commentary is both factual and personal.

Writer's checklist: commentaries

- Have you considered an aspect of everyday life in a balanced and thoughtful way?
- Have you researched its background and health effects?
- Have you included a personal anecdote or experience?
- Have you used a variety of appropriate tenses for each section?
- Have you used time and order expressions to make it easier for the reader to follow?

Editor's checklist

Check

- that your ideas are organised into paragraphs
- your spelling and use of capital letters
- punctuation, especially commas and dashes
- the grammar is correct – past tenses.

Final draft

Once you have finished your commentary, collect the commentaries from the class and publish them as a small booklet.

Check your progress

I can:	Needs more work	Almost there	All done!
write to analyse, review and comment			
comment on an aspect of everyday life in an interesting way			
use a variety of tenses for specific purposes			
use connectives to make my commentary clear.			

6 Between the lines

How can I reflect some of the different ways stories are told?

When you think of stories, you probably imagine them told in a fairly normal way – following the narrator's adventures or experiences as he or she describes them. But stories are told in many different ways – for example, through letters or emails from one character to another, or using **dual narrators** who alternate chapters, in diary form, or even in a series of tweets! Talk briefly with a friend about stories told in diary or letter form – what do you think are the advantages or disadvantages of each approach?

> ### Key term
>
> **dual narrators**: two different narrators, each telling their version of the story

Effective original narratives

A good narrative should:

- create a *vivid personal voice* through *first person* narration
- give a *convincing picture* of the narrator's situation
- use *the present tense* to create immediacy and drama
- *create empathy* for the narrator and his/her feelings through characterisation and events.

Reading

The following text is narrated by a young black girl in the southern states of the USA in the mid-nineteenth century. At that time, many rich white landowners kept slaves to work on their farms or in their houses. The writer of the extract you are about to read has tried to give her narrator a believable voice, so be aware that not all of the spellings or grammar are in standard English; instead, they reflect the accent, dialect and way of speaking of the time.

1 As you read the text, think about these questions:

a What impression do you get of Clotee (the slave girl telling the story) in this extract?

b What does the use of the diary form add to the story?

Next mornin', first light

I got up extra early and churned the butter for breakfast and helped out in the kitchen the way Aunt Tee 'spects me to every mornin'. That give me a little time to practice* my writin' at my spot by the big tree out behind the kitchen. Sunrise is a good writin' hour – when all is still and quiet.

I want to tell somebody, 'bout all the things I done learned for the past three years. Words got magic. Every time I read or write a word it puts a picture in my head.

Like when I write H-O-M-E I sees Belmont Plantation and all the people that live here. I sees the Big House where Mas' Henley, Miz Lilly and William stay, livin' easy. I sees the separate kitchen with the attic above it where I sleep along with Aunt Tee, Uncle Heb and Hince. I sees the Quarters where my friends live, and beyond their cabins, the fields and orchards where they work. I sees Aunt Tee cookin' at the fireplace, and the stables where Hince takes care of Mas' Henley's prize racin' horses, and the gardens and grounds that Uncle Heb makes pretty. Home. That one li'l word shows me all of that.

Mas' Henley thinks he owns everything here at Belmont, but he don't own all of me – not really. I know, he can tell me to come and I got to come. When he say do this, I better do it or he'll put the whip to my back. But I done learned that he cain't tell me what to think – and feel – and know.

He look at me every day but he cain't see what's in my head. He cain't own what's inside me. Nobody can.

Key language features
pronouns
parts of a place
apostrophes

Glossary

'spects: expects

plantation: large estate or farm growing crops such as cotton, sugar, tobacco, etc.

Mas': Master

Miz: Mistress

li'l: little

aine: (sounds like ain't) isn't

Few days later

It rained all the long, long day. Everything is dampish and sticky. I wondered if my diary stayed dry in its hidin' place. No need to worry, the stone covered it well.

Next day

It rained again today. When it rains hard, the field slaves don't have to work. But our work in the kitchen goes on all the time – no days off.

Aunt Tee say I'm lucky, gettin' picked to work in the Big House. I **aine** so sure. Livin' right under Mas' Henley and Miz Lilly aine so easy to me. We got to do their biddin', all hours of the night and day. But field work is hard – hard on your back, and in the summer, the heat is smothery. I guess what it comes to is bein' a slave aine no good no matter where they got you workin'.

Next day

I just wrote T-R-E-E. I see my tree – the live oak behind the kitchen where I come to write whenever I can slip away. I put a "s" on tree and now the word is trees. The picture in my head turns to the apple orchards. In spring, the apple trees are filled with bright, white blossoms. I close my eyes and see the same trees in the green of summer and full of good-tastin' apples in the fall. I love playin' with words – puttin' letters in and takin' letters out and lettin' the pictures change.

* (US spelling)

From *Slave Girl: An African-American Girl's Diary 1859* by Patricia C. McKissack

How the text works

Do you remember what makes a powerful, original narrative? Here is how the writer makes it work. She:

- creates a vivid personal voice through the strong, first person narration

- gives a convincing picture of Clotee's situation

- uses the present tense to create immediacy and drama

- uses the diary form to create empathy for the narrator and her feelings.

Text analysis

The extract comes from the opening to a novel, so the writer has a number of purposes:

- to establish Clotee's voice and character

- to give the reader some information about other people in the story

- to create drama and make us interested in what will happen

- to suggest some key themes or ideas.

1 In order to help you understand the first point above, try reading the extract aloud. The spellings ('caint' for 'can't' etc.) should help you with the accent. Are there any particular things she says that stand out when you read the extract? Why do they stand out or make an impact?

Reading closely

2 Look at the drawing below of the big house in the story. Reread the extract and then copy the image yourself (or work from a photocopy). Add/draw any further details about setting (e.g. the stables?) and write in the names of the people who live or work there.

3 Now, using what you have learned from the diagram and from rereading the text, answer these questions.

   a Where do Clotee (the narrator), Aunt Tee, Uncle Heb and Hince sleep/live?

   b What is the name for the buildings where Clotee's friends live?

   c What jobs do Hince and Uncle Heb do?

   d Why does Clotee think the 'field slaves' are luckier than she is?

   e Where does Clotee go to write her diary?

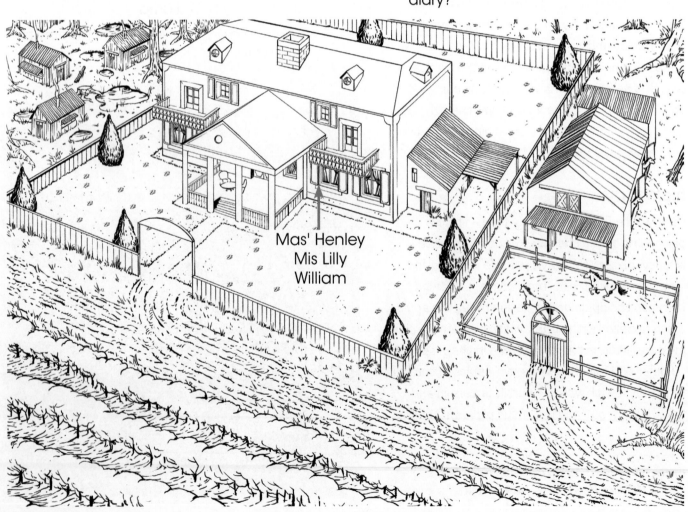

Mas' Henley
Mis Lilly
William

4 Clotee's powerful, personal voice is one of the most striking things about the extract, but how is this achieved? What do we find out about her? How does it make us feel as readers?

Working with a partner, look at the points in the table below and see if you can complete it.

a First, find a quotation from the extract that matches the point in the left-hand column. The first one has been done for you.

b Then, note the evidence.

c Finally, explain what this makes you think or feel about Clotee.

What we find out	• She is proud of her learning • She is defiant about her freedom • She is realistic about a slave's life • She is imaginative and inspired by writing
Evidence from text	'I want to tell somebody, 'bout all the things I done learned for the past three years.'
Effect or feeling created	Sad she can't share it with anyone. Impressed she has managed to teach herself to read.

5 The writer also uses a range of sentence lengths and types to create Clotee's voice.

a In the third paragraph, what repeated two-word phrase does she use at the start of several sentences, as she tells us what comes into her head when she writes 'HOME'?

b At the end of the short fifth paragraph she uses an **emphatic** short sentence to stress how independent she is. What is the short sentence?

Key term

emphatic: done or said in a strong way, without any doubt

Thinking about the text

Although Clotee is quite positive, this text has a more serious side to it.

6 Think carefully and then answer these questions.

a In an earlier part of the novel, Clotee reveals that the Master would 'beat the skin off' any of his slaves that he catches 'learning'. Why do you think the Master is so against the slaves being educated?

b Why do you think Clotee keeps a diary?

c What impression do you get of the Master from what Clotee says?

React to the text

7 Work in pairs. Discuss these questions.

a What sort of life do you think Clotee has? Is she happy or not? Why do you think this?

b What sort of life do you think it is for the slaves who work in the fields?

c How unusual or original do you find the story? What works well? Think about:

• the use of the diary form and style to tell it

• Clotee's voice and how distinctive it is

• anything else you like about it.

Use of English

Later in the unit you are going to write your own original story.

Pronouns: indefinite, relative, demonstrative

Grammar presentation

Remember that pronouns are used in place of a noun. There are indefinite pronouns (*something, nothing*), demonstrative pronouns (*this, that*), and relative pronouns (*that, which*). Writers use them a lot to avoid repeating words.

1 Match the underlined word in each sentence from the extract on pages 60–61 with the correct type of pronoun.

  a <u>That</u> give me a little time to practice my writin' at my spot by the big tree out behind the kitchen.

  i indefinite

  b I want to tell <u>somebody</u>, 'bout all the things I done learned for the past three years.

  ii demonstrative

  c I sees the Big House <u>where</u> Mas' Henley, Miz Lilly and William stay, livin' easy.

  iii relative

2 Complete a table like the one below with the words in the box. One of the words can be in two categories.

that	somebody	where
anyone	these	which	no one
none	everything	this
anywhere	those	when	whose

Indefinite	Relative	Demonstrative

3 Complete the extract from a story with the words from the box.

~~everyone~~	whose	it	nobody
these	that	where	that
this	anyone

When (a) ___everyone___ had gone out, I took the key (b) _____ I'd put under the rock behind my dad's shed.

(c) _____ was the only place

(d) _____ I knew

(e) _____ could see me. I gently pushed the loose board on the side of the shed (f) _____ my dad had been promising to fix for months.

(g) _____ was the last place that

(h) _____ would look. Behind it was the box, (i) _____ brass top had lost its shine, containing the photos.

(j) _____ were so precious to me. I gently turned the key…

Vocabulary: parts of a place

In any story the setting matters. It's important to give a detailed description of where the action takes place so that the reader can visualise the setting.

4 Look at this part of the extract on pages 60–61. Circle the words that are parts of the place Clotee is describing.

I sees the separate kitchen with the attic above it where I sleep along with Aunt Tee, Uncle Heb and Hince. I sees the Quarters where my friends live, and beyond their cabins, the fields and orchards where they work. I sees Aunt Tee cookin' at the fireplace, and the stables where Hince takes care of Mas', Henley's prize racin' horses, and the gardens and grounds that Uncle Heb makes pretty. Home.

5 Look at each list of words. Name the place in each case. Can you add two more words to each list?

a gym, staff room, art room, science lab

b escalator, car park, restrooms, shops

c screen, seats, popcorn stand, ticket office

6 Match each definition below to the correct word from Activity 4 or 5.

a A place where people used to cook over an open fire.

b People keep horses here.

c An area with a lot of fruit trees.

d A set of stairs that move up and down by electrical power.

e A large room with equipment for taking exercise.

Write your own definition of three more words. Don't give the answers. Swap your definitions with your partner and guess their words while they guess yours.

Use pictures of places and things to increase your vocabulary. Try to name all the things you see.

Punctuation: apostrophes

Apostrophes are used to indicate possession (*Ali's books*) or omission (*I'm = I am*). When writing spoken English, writers use apostrophes to show letters that are not pronounced.

7 Write the full forms of these sentences from spoken English.

a I'm writin' a story about a girl who's blind.

b She's just a li'l girl.

c He should've been watchin' out.

d They don't know anythin' 'bout it.

Guided writing

Write the beginning of a short story in which the main character hides something precious or dear to him/her. Write it from the point of view of the main character (in the first person) using a diary form. Give some information about the character's situation – where he/she is, what he/she does, etc. Imagine that your character is also learning something new, like Clotee in the story.

Note: You don't have to try to write how your character speaks – focus instead on writing an interesting narrative.

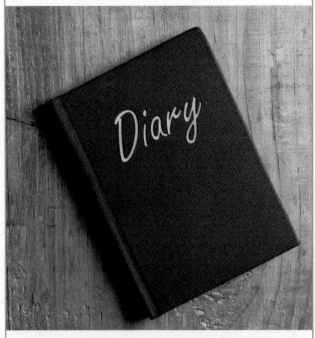

Write part of a short story in an original narrative style.

Think/Plan

1 Work in pairs. Generate ideas for your stories. Answer the questions to help you.

   a What has your character hidden? Why?

   b Where is the story set? Describe the place and other characters.

   c What is your character learning?

   d Can you think of a historical setting for your character?

2 Now plan three or four days of the diary. Some entries can be shorter than others. Take notes for each day. Note down the thoughts of your character on his/her learning. Use the following structure if you like.

   Day 1: describe the setting and what the character has hidden

   Day 2: a day when nothing happens but write about some of your character's thoughts

   Day 3: update about the character's learning and further details of other characters

   Day 4: describe an achievement (however small) by your character and what it means to him/her.

Write: day 1

Write the first entry of your diary.

Follow these steps.

a Give a 'voice' to your character: let us know where he/she is and what he/she does.

b Tell us about what your character has hidden, why and where.

c Introduce what he/she is learning and describe the first steps and how he/she feels.

d Describe the place in more detail and how the character interacts with it.

e Introduce other characters that your character meets or deals with.

Write: days 2 and 3

Take a break in the main action, for example your character is at home sick or on a day off.

a Describe briefly what your character is doing on these days.

b Use this 'break' to describe your character's thoughts or to develop other action. Explain, for example, why your character's learning is so important to him/her, or why he/she has hidden the object and why it is so dear to him/her.

c Use some of these ideas to help you:

- *There was no school today so I decided to…*

- *I felt a bit feverish this morning so I stayed in bed…*

- *It's Saturday but I've no plans. I've decided to…*

- *I spent the day practising…*

- *[Character] came to visit today. He/ She told my mother that…*

Write: finish the story

Now write the end of your story extract – the last diary entry.

a Describe something that your character achieves, however small, and how he/she feels about it.

b Explain how important it is for your character.

Things to remember when writing a narrative

- Use first person narrative for the voice for your character.

- Use a diary form to help readers relate to your character.

- Give a convincing picture of your character's situation.

- Include details about the setting.

- Use present tenses to create a sense of immediacy.

Check your first draft

When you have finished writing, be your own editor.

- Try reading your diary entries aloud to yourself. Then read them to your partner.

- Discuss how to improve the action and focus on the voice of your character.

- When you read aloud, you probably found some sentences that need improving. Work on these to make them sound better.

Peer assessment

Write your assessment of your partner's work in the form of three or four questions that require him/her to assess their own work and discuss the issues with you.

Now write a second draft of your diary entries.

Independent writing

Choose *one* of these ideas for a narrative form and write an original story of 350–400 words about *one* of the hidden objects.

Narrative form	Hidden object
Emails to a friend	A personal souvenir
	A gift from someone who has passed away
Letters	A letter from someone dear to you
Diary entries	
	Something valuable (ring, watch, necklace…)

Write at least three or four parts (diary entries, letters/emails).

Follow these stages.

Stage 1 Generate ideas for your character. Think about the setting, time, age, etc. Look back at the tip in the Guided writing section on things to give your character.

Stage 2 Put your ideas into a plan, using a timeline.

- Where is your character? What has he/she hidden?
- What is he/she learning or finding out?
- How does the action develop?
- What does he/she achieve in the end?

Stage 3 Write your story in the appropriate form for your narrative (letters, messages, diary entries, etc.), following your plan. Use the checklist below to make sure your narrative and character are original.

Writer's checklist: original narratives

- Have you chosen an original narrative form for your character?
- Have you created a voice for your character through the narrative form?
- Have you described his/her situation?
- Have you developed the action over the different entries/letters/messages, etc.?
- Have you used a variety of present tenses to give your narrative more immediacy?

Editor's checklist

Check

- that your ideas are organised into paragraphs
- your spelling and use of capital letters
- punctuation, especially apostrophes
- the grammar is correct – use of pronouns (indefinite, relative, demonstrative).

Final draft

Once you have finished your narrative, publish all the class's work as a magazine and distribute copies around the school.

Check your progress

I can:	Needs more work	Almost there	All done!
tell a narrative in an original way and sustain a character			
use an appropriate narrative form for your character's voice			
use the narrative form to create empathy for the narrator			
create a sense of immediacy through the language.			

7 More than a play

Your writing aim for this unit: To use dramatic structure to create impact

Writing objectives for first language English	Writing and Use of English objectives for second language English
In this unit, you will:	In this unit, you will:
• create and sustain character, viewpoint and voice	• use conditional structures
• select the most suitable layout and presentation to create impact	• learn environment collocations
• understand how writers adapt phrases, sentences and conventions to create effects.	• use correct punctuation – exclamations.

Key terms that you will learn: theme   dramatic conventions   symbolic   irony

How do I create a drama with a strong impact?

Think about an **issue** you feel strongly about and then in a group share your ideas. Decide on one idea (for example, greater isolation created by social media). What would be the best or most effective way to get people to think about your concerns? In a poem? A leaflet or poster? Would a play work – why or why not? Or something else? Jot down the **pros and cons** of each form as a way of sharing your views.

Glossary

issue: important subject or problem

pros and cons: advantages and disadvantages

Effective dramas with themes

A good **thematic** drama should:

- create a *strong impact* on an *audience*
- use **dramatic conventions** (staging, sound, design etc) to get the message across
- use *speech* and *dialogue* to express *powerful thoughts* or *feelings*
- be *set out* on the page in the *correct manner* with names on the left, no speech marks, etc.

Key terms

theme: the subject of a book, film or play

dramatic conventions: references in play scripts to key elements that create atmosphere and make the audience feel they are watching something real. For example, sound effects, set design, etc.

Reading

The following extract comes from a play about ecological issues. It is unlike other plays you may have read: there is no central character and the play is not like 'real life', but it does have a powerful message.

You could read it to yourself, or create a short performance in groups of 5–6 (one person reading the stage directions).

1 As you read the text, think about these questions:

   a There are two very different groups of characters in this extract: who are they – and how are they different?

   b What do you think the play is going to be about from reading this opening scene?

Path to the Future

Lights up on the stage. There is a twisting road which leads from one corner to its diagonal opposite. On the back wall, there is the image of a rainforest with a mountain towering above it. It is dark with gloomy clouds above it. The road seems to enter the forest. Enter a figure, SMOKE, in a grey hood. SMOKE stops, turns and gestures, as if beckoning others to follow him.

SMOKE: Come on, you lot! We haven't got all day.

Slowly, a series of other figures emerge. First, comes CAR, a box-like figure of shiny metal. Then comes POLLUTION, a slimy figure covered in oily marks and fishy green scales. Finally comes MONEY, wearing a suit of dollar bills.

POLLUTION: Oi, Smoke! I'm exhausted.

The others laugh, nastily.

MONEY: (*holding his nose*) 'Exhausted' – good, one Pollution! And don't stand so close – you stink.

POLLUTION: Call me, Poll. We've been together a long time.

SMOKE: What would you say, Poll, if I told you I've found the perfect place for us?

POLLUTION: I'd say it's about time.

SMOKE: What would you say, Car, if I told you this place was pure, beautiful and full of life?

CAR: (*snarling*) Horrible!

MONEY: (*recoiling*) Yuk!

POLLUTION: (*choking*) How disgusting!

SMOKE: What would you say if I told you *we* can turn it into something dirty, smelly and distorted? Wouldn't you like to gobble up whatever you like, Money – and get bigger and bigger? You, Car, wouldn't you like to go wherever you wanted, chopping down forests and clearing mountains to make roads? And wouldn't you like to contaminate the soil and all the pretty flowers and poison deep blue oceans, Pollution?

The others look at each other.

CAR: (*slightly apologetic*) I don't mean to be ungrateful Smoke, but … well, it seems too good to be true. Surely people will drive us out?

Key language features

conditional sentences

environment collocations

exclamations

Glossary

ecosystem: the biological network of species and organisms

omnipotent: all-powerful

MONEY:	'Drive' – good one, Car!
SMOKE:	Ok, enough with the jokes. I get your point, but that's just it. This place is full of people who *want* us to invade. Particularly the adults.
POLLUTION:	What's this place of yours called, then? And where is it?

SMOKE turns and points to the back wall.

SMOKE:	Ta-dah! They call it 'Earth'. Stupid name if you ask me. Quite a lot of it is sea and rock, but humans were never the most intelligent species. Best thing of all is, there's *no one* protecting its environment! No one to stop us! Come on. While it's dark, we can sneak in.

SMOKE marches up the road, but at that moment, the light suddenly changes. The sun comes up on the back wall, and there is the sound of birdsong. A small figure leaps out and blocks his path. It is a child of about ten years of age. He/she is CHILD OF THE FUTURE and he/she carries a long staff which they wield in front of them.

CHILD:	(*firmly*) Oh no you don't.
SMOKE:	(*shielding his eyes from the bright rays*) Oi, kid. Push off. You're in our way.
CHILD:	I know.
SMOKE:	(*uncertainly*) Err. Well, move.
CHILD:	No.

MONEY approaches, holding out dollar bills.

MONEY:	Surely you'd like a little bit of extra pocket money, kiddie, wouldn't you? All you have to do is turn your back and let us get on with destroying your **ecosystem**.
CHILD:	I said 'No'.
CAR:	Look. You're just one small, skinny kid. We're large and **omnipotent**. And nasty too.
CHILD:	I'm not alone.

At that moment, the forest behind CHILD OF THE FUTURE seems to part and other children emerge. They are all dressed like the first CHILD and each carries a long stick or pole.

Mike Gould

How the text works

Do you remember what makes a play with a strong theme? Here is how the writer makes it work. He:

- uses the dramatic structure to introduce **symbolic** figures (the polluting characters entering dressed in representative costumes)
- uses dramatic conventions to create impact (the set design of the rainforest on the backdrop)
- uses vocal patterns to make the drama poetic and memorable (for example, Smoke's rhetorical questions, the child's simple language)
- sets up conflict, which the audience wants to see resolved.

Key term

symbolic: representing something

Text analysis

1 The extract is the opening to a play. Openings usually:

- start the plot or story – what is going to happen? What problem or **obstacle** will the main character or characters have to overcome?

- create a mood or atmosphere through the setting or staging

- create style or **tone** through particular words, phrases, voices or sounds

- introduce some key themes or ideas that the playwright wants to explore.

In a group of five or six – perhaps the same group who performed the extract – divide a large sheet of paper into four sections, like the one below – and write as many ideas as you can about each of these aspects into the boxes. Some have been started for you.

Reading closely

2 The 'pollutant' figures at the start are dressed in ways which are representative of their 'character'

   a What shape is Car and why is he 'shiny'?

   b What is appropriate about Smoke's headwear?

   c How is Pollution's outfit appropriate?

   d Money makes two stupid puns both related to cars and their engines – what are they?

3 What is **ironic** about the reaction of the group to Smoke's offer of a 'pure, beautiful ... place'?

Plot/story	Mood/atmosphere – what is the setting or staging?
At first: *a group of nasty figures who represent ...* Later: *But ...*	At first: Later:
Style/tone – words, phrases or sounds	**Key themes or ideas**
At first: *rhetorical questions create tension. Jokes and puns which hide an unpleasant reality.* Later:	At first: *threats to beauty and nature which adults have done little to prevent.* Later:

Glossary

obstacle: something or someone that blocks your path – in a story this could be an enemy or rival

tone: feeling created by the language

irony: when someone says something which has an unintended, often contrasting meaning

4 'Smoke' tries to entice the others in several ways.

    a What does he say Car can do?

    b What do the words 'gobble up' suggest about the way Money would consume things?

    c What does Smoke offer Pollution?

5 The scene changes dramatically just before the end. The contrast is shown in both the stage directions and the way the characters speak.

    a What word meaning '*to get in the way of*' tells us what the child does in front of Smoke?

    b What tells us Smoke does not quite know what to do when the Child refuses to move?

    c What stage direction tells us Smoke finds the sun's glare painful?

Thinking about the text

The text has a clear message which is shown from the language, structure and style.

6 Think carefully and then answer these questions.

    The 'pollutants' speak in a number of ways which show they despise the Child.

    a What informal word meaning 'young person' or 'child' does Smoke use?

    b What phrase meaning 'go away' is also used?

7 How would you describe the way the four figures at the start are presented? Which of these adjectives suit their characterisation? Why?

thoughtful	kind	aggressive
greedy	sympathetic	powerful

8 At one point, Pollution says to Money, 'We've been together a long time'. On the surface, this means we've been friends or companions for a long time, but what more serious meaning could this have?

React to the text

9 Work in pairs. Discuss these questions.

    a In the play, the writer suggests that adults are to blame for 'inviting' harmful things onto our planet. Do you think this is true? In what ways?

    b Do you think it is fair to represent 'money' as something harmful? Why? Why not?

    c Have you ever felt angry about exploitation of natural resources – for example, how nature or the environment near you has been used or abused?

Use of English

Later in the unit you will write a scene from a play.

Conditional sentences

Grammar presentation

In the extract from the play on pages 70–71 the character called Smoke uses a conditional sentence which imagines a present situation that is hypothetical or unreal.

1 Look at this sentence from the play. Is this a first, second or third conditional structure? What tenses are used?

*What **would** you **say**, Car, if I **told** you this place was pure, beautiful and full of life?*

2 Look at the following sentences. Say which conditional form each one is and what tenses are used.

 a If we clear this land, we will be able to build a factory.

 b If we had more land, we would be able to grow more crops.

 c If we had bought more land last year, we would have planted more crops.

3 Choose the correct option to complete these conditional sentences.

 a If we *didn't look / don't look* after our planet, we will destroy it.

 b If we use drift nets, we *would / will* be able to catch more fish.

 c The climate *won't / wouldn't* have changed if we hadn't burned so much fossil fuel.

 d If we *had protected / protected* the natural world, a lot of animals wouldn't have died out.

 e If we continue dumping chemicals into the sea, it *will / would* threaten all sea life.

 f We wouldn't produce so much waste if everyone *recycled / had recycled* more.

4 Complete each of the following sentences with the correct form of the verb in brackets. Then decide who might say this, the Child (C) or the Polluters (P).

 a If you chop down all of this forest, the world's climate _____ (damage).

 b If you _____ (not be) so greedy, Money, you wouldn't be destroying the planet.

 c We need cars – if we don't have cars, we _____ (not have) smoke and pollution.

 d We _____ (destroy) everything if those children hadn't got in our way.

 e How _____ (you grow) anything if you contaminate the soil?

Vocabulary: environment collocations

Vocabulary presentation

The main theme of the play on pages 70–71 is our environment and protecting the planet. There are many verb-noun collocations (words that commonly go together) related to the environment.

5 Complete this line from the play extract with the correct verbs.

You, Car, wouldn't you like to go wherever you wanted, _____ forests and _____ mountains? And wouldn't you like to _____ the soil and all the pretty flowers and _____ deep blue oceans, Pollution?

6 Match the verbs and nouns to make more collocations related to the environment.

a	chop down	**i**	natural resources
b	protect	**ii**	fossil fuels
c	recycle	**iii**	the environment
d	deplete	**iv**	the air
e	pollute	**v**	trees
f	burn	**vi**	waste

7 Complete this extract from the play with the correct form of the words from Activities 5 and 6.

SMOKE: I just want to **(a)** _____ the air because I love **(b)** _____ fossil fuels.

POLLUTION: Yeah, all we want to do is **(c)** _____ your whole ecosystem.

CHILD: No! I can't let you do that. I'm here to **(d)** _____ the environment.

MONEY: But why can't I just **(e)** _____ this land here and build houses?

CHILD: Because it's protected.

CAR: Protected?

MONEY: Listen, kid. We just want to **(f)** _____ some trees. What do you care?

CHILD: Because if we continue **(g)** _____ our natural resources, there'll be nothing left.

Tip

When you're learning vocabulary, don't just focus on individual words. Focus on collocations with verbs and nouns, adjectives and nouns, verbs and prepositions, etc.

Punctuation: exclamations

Punctuation presentation

Exclamations are words or short phrases that show humour or strong emotions such as surprise, anger, pain, excitement or even violence; or words or phrases that are meant to be spoken loudly. We indicate the exclamation by using an exclamation mark at the end.

8 Which of these words, phrases or sentences are exclamations? Insert an exclamation mark at the end if they are.

a Chop down the rainforest.

b What a fantastic idea.

c The sky is blue.

d Ha. You must be joking.

e How amazing.

Guided writing

You have been commissioned to write a new stage adaptation of *Path to the Future*. Write the next scene of the play in which the Children sit down with Money, Smoke, Car and Pollution. The Children try to make the polluting characters see all the damage they are doing to Earth and what a beautiful place it would be without them.

Write the next scene from the play.

Think/Plan

1 Work in pairs. Generate ideas for the scene. Answer the questions to help you.

a How do the Children behave? How do they speak?

b How do the polluting characters behave? What do they say?

c How do the Children explain to each character what they are doing to Earth?

d What is the other characters' reaction?

Tip

You could use the table you saw in the Text analysis section on page 72 to generate ideas for your scene.

2 Now plan the action in the scene. Use some of these ideas if you like.

- The Children explain to Car how our cities have been taken over by cars and how they cause air pollution. Car promises to change.

- The Children explain to Smoke and Pollution where they come from and the damage that has been done to the atmosphere, environment and oceans. Smoke and Pollution promise to get clean.

- Money doesn't want to change because he has all the power and controls everything. The Children convince him that he can still grow with a clean planet.

Useful language

Phrases: *If we chop down these forests…, Let's clear this mountain…, We have to protect our interests…, Think what could be done if we…, A clean planet benefits everyone…, If you hadn't polluted the air…, If you think about what will happen in the future…*

Environment: *destroy the ecosystem, poison the oceans, contaminate the soil, chop down forests, protect the environment, recycle waste, deplete natural resources, pollute the air, burn fossil fuels*

Write: set the scene

Write the description of the scene. Describe what is happening on the stage when the scene starts.

Use italics and include some information about:

- lights and any spotlights
- music and sounds
- special effects (for example, mist)
- who is on stage or who comes on (*Enter …*)
- costumes.

Write: dialogue

Write the dialogue.

Include the following ideas:

- conditional sentences: predictions about the future; speculation about current situation; speculation about past situations
- exclamations
- vocabulary related to the environment.

Here's an idea to get you started:

SMOKE: But cars, trucks, and factories produce smoke – there's nothing you can do about it.

CHILD: Oh, but there is. We can make cars and trucks that don't produce smoke and we can ask factories to reduce the amount of smoke they **emit**.

SMOKE: But that's not fair. What will happen to me if you make clean cars and trucks?

CHILD: Look at our cities, Smoke. The air is full of dirty, choking, black smoke. It hurts our lungs and causes terrible illnesses.

SMOKE: Illnesses? … That's a lie!

Glossary

emit: send out smoke, pollution or gas

Finish the story

At the end of the scene, the Children convince Money that he can prosper and develop without the other characters. Money joins forces with the Children to get rid of the polluting characters.

- The Children take Money aside and show him clean energy and people planting trees and cleaning the oceans. He realises he can still grow with these new ideas.
- Money decides to work with the Children and help them.
- Car becomes cleaner and Smoke and Pollution disappear.

Things to remember when writing a scene

- Describe the stage when the scene starts. Use italics.
- Use speech and dialogue to express emotions.
- Set out the dialogue using the correct format.
- Use dramatic conventions to introduce symbolic figures, with their own speech patterns.

Check your first draft

When you have finished writing, be your own editor.

- Read your scene aloud, or ask your friends to help you to act out the scene.
- Listen to how it sounds and think about how it will look.
- Add or take out parts as necessary to make sure the action progresses.

Now write a second draft of your scene.

Peer assessment

Read your partner's scene, focusing on the dialogue. Decide whether the characters are sustained and consistent in how they speak and act.

Independent writing

Write a scene from a play of 350–400 words.

Choose *one* of these ideas.

- A village has one well, which supplies all the villagers with water, but a rich man/woman who owns the land wants sole use of it.

- In a forest the animals live safe and free, but now hunters have come for food and fur.

- A family of orangutans lives in the rainforest but now diggers and bulldozers driven by farmers have moved in to clear the land to plant palm trees.

Write a full scene with stage directions and a set of several opposing characters.

Follow these stages.

Stage 1 Generate ideas. Think of different characters on the opposing sides and what they want.

Stage 2 Put your ideas into a plan, using the table you used in the Guided writing section.

- What is the basic story of the play? What scene are you writing?

- Where does the scene take place?

- What happens in the scene?

Stage 3 Write your scene using the appropriate dramatic conventions, following your plan. Use the checklist to make sure your scene creates impact.

Writer's checklist: creating drama

- Have you created interesting, symbolic figures to convey your message?

- Have you used the correct conventions and format for your scene?

- Have you used these dramatic conventions to create an impact?

- Do your characters use speech patterns to make the drama more poetic and memorable?

- Have you used shorter, violent sentences and exclamations for the 'villain(s)' and longer, more thoughtful lines for the 'heroes'?

Editor's checklist

Check

- that your dialogue is organised on separate lines according to who is speaking

- that you have indicated clearly who is speaking

- your spelling and use of capital letters

- punctuation, especially exclamation marks

- the grammar is correct – conditional sentences.

Final draft

Once you have finished your scene, work in a group and act it out for the class.

Check your progress

I can:	Needs more work	Almost there	All done!
establish and sustain different characters with their own points of view and voice			
use the appropriate format and conventions to write a scene from a play and create an impact			
adapt language and sentence structures to create different effects.			

8 Making yourself heard

Your writing aim for this unit: To write a speech for a specified audience

Writing objectives for first language English	Writing and Use of English objectives for second language English
In this unit, you will:	In this unit, you will:
• create and sustain a clear and logical viewpoint using convincing evidence, opinions and information	• learn expressions for making suggestions
• write arguments that develop in a clear way.	• use prepositions following verbs
• develop your use of language in paragraphs, and structure ideas between them, to achieve particular effects.	• use cohesion – addition and contrast connectives.

Key terms that you will learn: rhetorical question   thesis statement

How do I get ideas across in a speech in a clear and persuasive way?

This unit is about writing a speech that will argue a particular point of view. However, you may also be asked to read or present the speech you write. So, what physical and vocal skills do you think are needed if you are giving a presentation or a speech to a group of people? Write down your 'top five' (for example, Speak clearly) and then compare them with a friend's or partner's. Did either of you miss out anything important?

Effective speeches

A good speech expressing a point of view should:

- have a *clear structure*: introduction, main points, conclusion and 'call to action'
- develop an *argument point by point*
- use *language* that is *appropriate* for the *audience*
- contain some *language devices* designed to *persuade* listeners.

Glossary

vocal: to do with the voice

call to action: an appeal to the listener to do something

Reading

The following speech was given by a student representative. She has been asked to give her views to the **school council** on whether the annual school sports day needs to be changed or improved.

1 As you read the text, think about these questions:

   a What is the speaker's general view about the current sports day?

   b How would you sum up her main suggestions?

Sport for all?

Hello – and thank you for inviting me to address you on the issue of whether our sports day is suitable for all students or needs improving. This is an issue both for you, my fellow students, and for staff, some of whom are sitting here today. I am going to talk about what Sports Day is like at the moment, and then move on to how I think it could be improved.

Firstly, I want to **recap** briefly how annual Sports Day works now. Currently, we have an afternoon in the summer when the form classes/tutor groups from each year group choose teams and compete in a variety of activities. These consist of quite a narrow range of traditional events such as individual track-based running and **relay** races (100 metres, 400 metres), as well as a small number of **field events** such as long jump, high jump and **discus** throwing. Individual prizes (and points) are only awarded for first, second and third places, though an overall trophy goes to the form or team with the highest number of points in each year group.

This works very well if you like athletics, but there are a lot of students who take part and never win, and even more who do not participate at all. This is a great shame as Sports Day could include many more events that would engage students' interests. 'Sport' does not have to mean traditional races or activities where physical **prowess** is the only measure of success. For a start, why not include some of the silly, fun games we used to play at primary school such as the 'egg and spoon' race or the three-legged race? Just because we are older now, this does not mean we wouldn't enjoy these activities. What is more, these events still require skill – even if the outcome, falling over in a heap or the egg going flying in the air, is often comical!

In addition, I would recommend having a wider range of proper sports or games students can take part in. There could be chess tournaments, table-tennis competitions, or **pool** games. Or we could include popular games such as five-a-side football or basketball. Isn't it the case that most students would find *something* they enjoy? Perhaps you are thinking of games as I speak right now. Indeed, part of the planning could be to put together a questionnaire asking students what games or sports they would like to include and then select the most popular ones. Who knows, there may be huge numbers of students out there who love racing on skateboards or playing **darts**!

Nevertheless, there may still be students who feel that these activities are unsuitable for them, or who get stressed out at the thought of any form of competitive game. It is vital we **cater** for them too, so I would suggest they help

with the organisation of the day, whether that is in helping set up the racing areas, putting seating out or if parents are attending, showing them where to sit or selling refreshments. Others would do a brilliant job as referees, ball-boys or girls, or assistants to the teachers. We could even create a student 'press pack' of photographers and reporters who could write up events for the school magazine or website.

The key thing is for us to create activities that everyone can contribute to in some way, big or small. It may be true that some staff, perhaps even some here today, would like to get rid of Sports Day altogether because of its competitive nature, but I think that would be a mistake. Plenty of students enjoy competing whether they win or lose, and if there are lots of alternatives for those who are not particularly competitive, then it's a 'win-win' for all concerned.

Finally, I'd like to leave you with a vision of what Sports Day could look like. Imagine a sunny afternoon. Student **stewards** in neat uniforms show parents to their seats as they gather to watch their children compete. In front of them on the grassy track, some students are warming up for a 100-metre sprint, but on the other side of the painted white lines is a trampoline where students are practising fancy spins and **outrageous** tumbles. Nearby, there are neat rows of tables where students are facing each other across chess boards, pawns at the ready. Everyone is involved. Who could argue against that?

This could be our Sports Day next year. If we don't take this opportunity, then we risk disappointing hundreds of students. I hope we can all make it happen! Thank you for listening.

Key language features

making suggestions

verb + preposition

addition and contrast

Glossary

school council: a group of people, usually consisting of teachers and student representatives (often elected by classes)

recap: to repeat the key points

relay: running race in which one runner passes a baton to another in his or her team to continue the race

field events: events such as discus, hammer, long jump, high jump and triple jump, which measure the distance or height someone achieves

discus: a heavy disc that competitors have to swing and throw as far as they can

prowess: skill or ability

pool: a game played on a table, similar to snooker, where the objective is to clear the table of all your balls

darts: game where competitors throw a set of three sharp, pointed objects (darts) at a round, numbered board

cater: provide

stewards: people whose job it is to assist or guide large crowds

outrageous: shocking (meant here in a good way)

How the text works

Do you remember what makes a good persuasive speech? Here is how the writer made it work. She:

- introduced her speech and set out what her subject was

- developed her argument by suggesting lots of linked points, ending with a call to action

- engaged with her audience through direct address and **rhetorical questions**

- used other persuasive devices (such as creating images) to get her message across

- used an appropriate tone for the audience of staff and students.

Key term

rhetorical question: a question that makes a point by assuming an answer ('Do you really want to go out in this terrible rain?' The speaker assumes the answer will be 'no'.)

Text analysis

1 The speech works partly because of the way the argument progresses. Two key elements of this are the summary of what Sports Day is currently like, and the vision of what it could be like.

   a Where can you find these two sections in the speech?

   b Why do you think the speaker chose to put them in these positions in the speech?

Reading closely

2 The speech is divided into eight paragraphs in total. The idea is that it builds up and becomes more persuasive as it develops. Work in small groups of 4–5 and discuss the table below before copying and completing it. There is no absolute 'right' answer to column 3 but you should discuss what score it should get and why. For example, in paragraph 2 the speaker says the activities are 'quite narrow'. This is negative and suggests the activities could be more varied.

Paragraph	Focus	How persuasive? (1 – low; 10 – high)
1	Introduction – reason for speech	1 – no persuasion at this point.
2	What Sports Day is like currently	4–5? – says activities are 'quite narrow'
3		
4		
5		
6		
7		
8	Conclusion – with 'call to action'	

3 The persuasive language and devices are key to the success of the speech. Work on your own to look again closely at the text. Some of these answers may have come up in your discussion for the previous task.

   a Can you identify three rhetorical questions designed to make the audience agree?

   b The argument is also helped by the use of connectives at the start of paragraphs to develop and emphasise ideas.

     i What adverb meaning 'To begin with' is used near the beginning of the speech?

     ii What phrase meaning 'Also' is used in the middle of the speech?

     iii What word meaning 'in spite of' or 'all the same' is used at the start of one of the paragraphs?

     iv What adverb meaning 'Lastly' is used towards the end of the speech?

   c The writer addresses the audience directly on a number of occasions. Find at least two examples. What is the effect?

Thinking about the text

How persuasive are the writer's arguments?

4 Think carefully and then answer these questions.

   a What arguments does the speaker make? Copy out the barometer and each time you locate an argument in the text, point your finger at the barometer to show if the point is a good or bad one. Try to explain why.

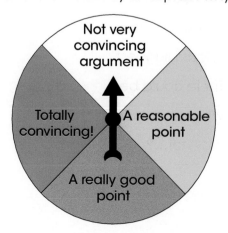

b How would you describe the tone of the speech as a whole?

   i Polite but persuasive

   ii Rude and aggressive

   iii Funny and silly

   iv Serious and neutral

React to the text

5 Work in pairs. Discuss these questions.

   a In the speech, the speaker says that some people don't think Sports Day should exist at all. What do you think?

   b How important is competition in schools? Is it something to be welcomed or is it problematic?

   c In what ways is the speech effective in persuading the council that Sports Day needs changing?

Use of English

Later in the unit you will write a speech.

Making suggestions

Grammar presentation

When you make a speech, you are trying to persuade the audience of something. This involves making suggestions. We can do this by using different structures.

1 Look at these sentences from the speech on pages 80–81. Which phrases are used to make suggestions? What verb form is used: gerund or infinitive?

   a For a start, why not *include* some of the silly, fun games…

   b I would recommend *having* a wider range of proper sports…

   c …we could *include* popular games…

2 Here are some other expressions used to make suggestions. Complete each sentence with the correct verb from the box. Which one is a gerund and which one is not an infinitive?

> propose   giving   write
>
> take   hold

   a We could even _____ a referendum at school so students could vote on the issue.

   b Why don't we _____ a proposal for the school board?

   c Let's _____ an alternative idea to the rest of the class.

   d I would suggest that we _____ a vote on this issue first.

   e How about _____ students more time to decide?

3 Choose the correct verb forms to complete the speech.

Firstly, I would recommend that we **(a)** *explain / to explain* to parents why we have decided to take this step. So, we could **(b)** *sending / send* out an informative letter to parents explaining the new policy. I would also recommend **(c)** *introduce / introducing* the policy gradually in the final term. Let's **(d)** *talk / to talk* to the teachers, and we could even **(e)** *inviting / invite* some parents to a meeting. Why don't we **(f)** *get / to get* everyone involved because it's such an important issue?

4 Complete the sentences with your own ideas about a sports day in your school.

   a Why don't we…

   b I would suggest…

   c There could be…

   d What about…?

   e Why not…?

Vocabulary: verbs + prepositions

Vocabulary presentation

When explaining an issue or your point of view, you have to use verbs with dependent prepositions. Always learn them together.

5 Which prepositions follow these verbs? Check your answers in the speech on pages 80–81.

   a thank you _____

   b talk _____

   c compete _____

   d consist _____

6 Copy and complete the table with the verbs from the box. Sometimes there is more than one possible answer.

succeed	belong	insist
apologise	vote	invest
reply	depend	believe
prepare	result	concentrate
substitute	explain	comment

for	on
to	**in**

7 Choose the correct preposition to complete each sentence.

   a I'd like to thank you all *to / for* coming to our debate today.

   b Perhaps the school could invest *on / in* some new sports equipment.

   c Many students would like to compete *in / for* other competitions.

   d We shouldn't insist *with / on* making students do sports.

   e After that, I'm going to move on *to / for* the issue of sports injuries.

   f Before finishing I'd like to comment *of / on* a related issue.

Cohesion: connectives – addition and contrast

Cohesion presentation

In public speaking, it's important to structure your talk and to signal to your audience what you are doing next. You can use connectives or linking expressions to do this. Look at these examples from the speech on pages 80–81.

Connective	What it is doing
In addition, I would recommend having a wider range of proper sports or games students can take part in.	Signals you are adding another point to your argument
Nevertheless, there may still be students who feel that these activities are unsuitable for them, or who get stressed out at the thought of any form of competitive game.	Signals you are making a point that contrasts with the previous point

8 Look at the list of connectives. Are they used to add (A) or contrast (C)?

   a On the other hand

   b Furthermore

   c However

   d Additionally

   e As well as that

   f Even so

   g What is more

Guided writing

You are taking part in a school debate. The title (or **motion**) of the debate is:

**Homework should be banned
in all schools.**

In a traditional debate, there are two teams: one argues for the motion and the other argues against it. Choose which side you are on – it doesn't have to be what you personally believe (in fact, sometimes it is more fun to defend the side you don't actually support!).

Write a speech outlining and defending your team's position on this motion.

Glossary

motion: a formal suggestion that is discussed and voted on at a debate or meeting

Think/Plan

1 Work in pairs. Generate ideas for your speech. Copy the table below and complete it with different arguments and examples.

In favour of ban	Against ban

Tip

For a speech like this, it helps to consider both sides of the debate so that you can predict what the opposing side will say.

2 Now think of your **thesis statement**. This is a statement summarising in one sentence what you are arguing. It helps to give your thesis statement in your introduction. Use these ideas to help you:

- *I'm going to talk today about...*
- *My firm belief is that... because...*
- *My contention is that... because...*
- *I am going to argue that...*

Key term

thesis statement: a sentence that summarises your key point in an argument or debate

Useful language

Phrases: *Thank you for inviting me to address you on the issue of ..., This issue concerns us all., I'm going to start by talking about... and then move on to..., Firstly, I want to recap briefly, I would recommend..., Why not...?, Finally, I'd like to leave you with..., Thank you for listening.*

Verb + preposition: *compete with, consist of, succeed in, belong to, insist on, apologise for, vote on, invest in, reply to, depend on, believe in*

Write: opening

Write the opening of your speech.

In a speech – even more than in a piece of writing – it's very important to capture the audience's attention from the start.

Follow these steps.

- First, greet the audience (*Hello, Good morning everyone...*).

- Thank the audience for attending the debate.

- Present the motion (*Today's debate is on...; The motion today is...*).

- Give your thesis statement.

- Give a brief outline of your speech (*I'm going to start by talking about..., Then I'll move on to..., And finally...*).

Tip

Good public speakers often use a 'hook' to capture the audience's attention. Here are some examples:

Ask a question or ask for a show of hands:

- *How many people here...?*

Give a fact or statistic:

- *Recent research shows that...*

Make a provocative statement:

- *Homework is both unnecessary and useless.*

Write: continue your speech

Write the main part of your speech.

Follow these steps.

- Give three main points supporting your point of view.

- Give examples to illustrate your points.

- Talk directly to your audience: use imperatives, use rhetorical questions, use the second person plural, make suggestions.

- Try to anticipate what the other team will reply to your points.

Write: finish the speech

Now write the end of your speech.

Follow these steps.

- Present an image of what school would be like with your vision of life with or without homework.

- Use a rhetorical question to reinforce your point (for example, *Who could argue against that?*).

- Thank the audience for listening and end with a call to action.

Things to remember when writing a speech

- Have a clear structure.

- Capture the audience's attention and try to keep it by addressing them directly.

- Use persuasive language and illustrate your points with examples.

- Use connectives and linking words to structure your points.

- Use the appropriate tone for your audience.

Check your first draft

When you have finished writing, be your own editor.

- Check your speech against your outline of the main points.

- Read your speech aloud and make notes on the parts that were difficult to say or that weren't very persuasive.

- Discuss with your partner how to improve those parts.

Now write a second draft of your speech.

Peer assessment

Work in pairs or small groups and practise your speech. Give your partners feedback about clarity and pronunciation.

Independent writing

Write a speech of 350–400 words.
Choose *one* of these ideas.

- You are running for class president/head boy/girl at your school. Write a speech outlining your ideas and try to convince your fellow students to vote for you.
- You have been asked to make a speech to students, staff and parents about an issue or event at your school (school lunches, the school play).
- You are a member of the debating team and you are taking part in a debate, the motion for which is: *Physical education should be compulsory for both students and staff until the end of high school.*

Write a speech with at least three main points supporting your view.

Follow these stages.

Stage 1 Generate ideas. Work in pairs or small groups and brainstorm points for your speech. Discuss your thesis statement.

Stage 2 Put your ideas into a plan, using a table or grid.

- What is your thesis statement?
- What are your three main arguments? What examples are you going to give?
- What is your conclusion and call to action?

Stage 3 Write your speech in paragraphs, following your plan. Use the checklist to make sure your speech is persuasive enough.

Writer's checklist: speeches

- Have you built up a convincing argument?
- Do your arguments have a linked progression?
- Have you got a clear structure?
- Do you engage your audience by addressing them directly?
- Have you used persuasive language to get your message across?
- Do you end your speech with a convincing call to action?

Editor's checklist

Check

- that your speech is organised into distinct sections
- your spelling and use of capital letters
- cohesion – your use of connectives and linking words
- the grammar is correct – making suggestions, pronouns, etc.

Final draft

Once you have finished your speech, stand in front of your class and present it – without reading from your notes as much as possible. Take a class vote on the best speech.

Check your progress

I can:	Needs more work	Almost there	All done!
establish and sustain a clear point of view with convincing evidence, opinions and information			
organise my arguments with a good progression			
shape and craft language to persuade an audience			
make the speech clear with the use of addition and contrast connectives and linking devices.			

9 Writing about poetry

Your writing aim for this unit: To write a thoughtful response to a poem

Writing objectives for first language English	Writing and Use of English objectives for second language English
In this unit, you will: • learn to use writing to analyse, review and comment • extend your range of language and use it appropriately • understand how writers change phrase and sentence structures and conventions in their writing.	In this unit, you will: • learn how to use adverbs • learn reporting verbs • use correct punctuation – quotations.

Key terms that you will learn: critical   subject matter   interpretation

How do I explain my ideas about a text I have read?

This unit is about *how* you explain your ideas about a poem in writing. You will start by exploring a poem, then you will read what one student has written about it and explore the skills they have demonstrated. But before you begin, jot down 2–3 things you might be asked about a poem (think back to other units where you have studied poetry).

Effective critical responses

A good **critical** response should:

- *explain* the main **subject matter** of the poem (its story, themes, etc.)
- *explore* possible *meanings* or **interpretations**
- set out your *points* in a *clear way* and support them with *evidence*
- use accurate *poetic terms* or *references* to show you know what you are talking about
- give some sense of your *personal engagement* or *interest* in the poem.

> ### Key terms
>
> **critical**: expressing an opinion or judgement on something
>
> **subject matter**: what something is about
>
> **interpretation**: a suggested idea based on evidence (not a guess)

Reading

The following poem deals with a childhood experience.

1 As you read the text, think about these questions:

   a What, if anything, happens to the child in the poem?

   b Who is narrating the poem?

Punishment in Kindergarten

Today the world is a little more my own.
No need to remember the pain
A blue-**frocked** woman caused, throwing
Words at me like pots and pans, to drain
That honey-coloured day of peace.
'Why don't you join the others, what
A **peculiar** child you are!'

On the lawn, in **clusters**, sat my
schoolmates sipping
Sugarcane, they turned and laughed;
Children are funny things, they laugh
In **mirth** at others' tears, I buried
My face in the sun-warmed hedge
And smelt the flowers and the pain.

The words are muffled now, the laughing
Faces only a blur. The years have
Sped along, stopping briefly
At beloved **halts** and moving
Sadly on. My mind has found
An adult peace. No need to remember
That picnic day when I lay hidden
By a hedge, watching the steel-white sun
Standing lonely in the sky.

Kamala Das

> ### Glossary
>
> **frock**: a dress
> **peculiar**: strange
> **clusters**: groups of things
> **mirth**: happiness
> **halts**: places

Now read the first two paragraphs of a response by a student, Samira, to a question on the poem. She was asked: what ideas about childhood does the poet explore?

> The poem is mainly about how certain childhood experiences stay with you, even as you get older and become more confident. For example, the poet starts by saying in the first line how 'the world is a little more my own'. The use of the phrase 'my own' suggests that the poet feels she belongs in the world and is not so much of an outsider.
>
> The third line onwards explains how the poet remembers in particular the 'blue-frocked woman'. This woman said she was 'peculiar' for not playing with the other children, and this has stuck in her mind. The adult's words were obviously very hurtful as the poet uses a simile to say they hit her 'like pots and pans'.

Key language features

adverbs

reporting verbs

quotations

How the text works

Do you remember what makes a good critical response? Here is how the writer makes it work. She:

- makes a clear point in the topic sentence of the first paragraph ('The poem is mainly about...')

- uses evidence from the poem in the form of quotations to back up what she says

- analyses some of the key words or phrases

- uses the correct terms to talk about the poem ('line', 'verse', etc.)

- gives an interpretation of the poem (what it *might* be saying).

Text analysis

The two paragraphs of the critical response each contain three main elements:

- the main point the student is making (usually in the first topic sentence)

- evidence from the poem to support the main point (inside quotation marks)

- an explanation of the words or phrases from the poem plus, in one paragraph:

- a further explanation or interpretation.

1 Work with a partner on a copy of the two paragraphs from page 91 to:

  - highlight in one colour or underline the main point in each paragraph

  - circle any evidence (words taken from the original poem)

  - put a tick next to any explanation and a double-tick next to further explanation or interpretation.

Then, share what you have found with another pair. Do you agree on how the paragraphs have been constructed?

Tip

When you give an interpretation in a response, it can be useful to use verbs such as 'suggest' or 'imply' or modal forms such as 'it might mean that...'. For example, 'the poet suggests that memories can be painful.'

Reading closely

2 The student, Samira, mentions the simile of 'words...like pots and pans' but she has not explained why this is an effective simile. Which of these could be added to make the point even better?

The adult's words were obviously very hurtful as the poet uses a simile to say they hit her 'like pots and pans'. This is a good comparison because...

a pots and pans come from a kitchen and children are always in the kitchen

b pots and pans make a lot of noise when they are thrown and they are heavy metal objects

c pots and pans are probably things the woman is holding when she is in the playground

d pots and pans remind the girl of washing-up, which she doesn't like.

Remember: when you are *interpreting* a line's meaning, you are not guessing. For example, is there any evidence anywhere that the girl 'doesn't like washing up'? No – so **d** can't be right.

Before you can write about the rest of the poem in the same way as Samira, you will need to understand how it develops.

3 The second verse is about what the other children are doing and how they respond.

   a Where are they and what are they doing?

   b Why does the poet say children are 'funny things'?

   c How does the poet try to hide her face and tears?

4 The final verse seems to be about a different time. The poet says:

The words are muffled now, the laughing

Faces only a blur.

Which two words suggest the memory is not very clear?

Thinking about the text

What exactly is the poet saying about childhood?

5 Think carefully and then answer these questions.

   a How does the poet feel now in her life? What words or phrases tell you this?

   b How quickly has time passed?

   c She repeats a phrase from the first verse in the last verse – what is it? What do you think she is telling herself?

React to the text

6 Work in pairs. Discuss these questions.

   a Do you have any distinct memories of when you were a much smaller child in school? What are they?

   b How did you feel at the time? How do you feel now?

   c What do you think Kamala Das's main feelings about the childhood memory are? Choose one or more of the following and argue your view with a partner.

     i Angry about what happened

     ii Laughing over being so silly

     iii Sad about how she felt at the time

     iv Glad she has put it all behind her

     v Unconcerned – it didn't mean anything

   d How effective is Kamala Das's poem about childhood? How does she:

     • paint a picture

     • convey her own feelings

     • show contrast between past and present?

Use of English

Later in the unit you will write a response to the final part of the poem 'Punishment in Kindergarten'.

Adverbs

Grammar presentation

Adverbs are often used to modify a verb or to emphasise an element in a sentence. This type of sentence adverb can be used to qualify your meaning when giving an opinion.

1 Look at the following sentences. Explain what the underlined adverbs emphasise in the sentence.

  a The poem is <u>mainly</u> about how certain childhood experiences stay with you, <u>even</u> as you get older and become more confident.

  b The adult's words were <u>obviously</u> very hurtful…

2 Choose the correct adverb to complete each sentence.

  a This memory is *particularly / mainly* important to the author.

  b This image comes up several times in the poem, *usually / especially* in the third and fourth verses.

  c The author is *evidently / hopefully* remembering an important moment of her childhood.

  d The first verse *briefly / shortly* mentions the moment that is described later on.

  e *Consequently / Frankly* the poet feels alienated as a result of her origin.

3 Write each sentence with the adverb in the correct place. Sometimes there is more than one possible answer.

  a The poet is upset about what happened. (apparently)

  b The event is stuck in the author's memory. (evidently)

  c The woman doesn't consider this to be of any importance. (even)

  d The writer uses this word once in the first verse. (only)

  e It seems the poet doesn't believe this to be true. (actually)

Vocabulary: reporting verbs

Vocabulary presentation

In a response to a poem (or any other piece of writing), we report and comment on what the poet says. To do this we should use a range of different verbs.

4 Look at these sentences from the response to the poem. Which one reports on the use of language? Which reporting verbs are used?

  a …the poet starts by saying in the first line how…

  b The use of the phrase 'my own' suggests that…

5 Complete each sentence with the correct reporting verb. Sometimes there is more than one possible answer.

> wonders   insists   claims
>
> discusses   asks   tells
>
> reveals   explains

a The poem _____ the importance of our childhood memories.

b In the third line, the poet _____ that she didn't have a happy childhood.

c In the last verse, the poet _____ why she can't remember the details.

d The word 'pain' _____ us that not everything was positive.

e The old man in the first verse _____ he didn't know anything about love.

Tip

As you write your response, make sure you aren't repeating the same reporting verb (for example, *the poet says*).

Punctuation: quotations

Punctuation presentation

In a response, we also have to quote words, phrases and lines from the poem. Pay attention to the punctuation.

- Use single quotations: *The word 'peculiar' suggests…*

- Commas and full stops always go inside the quotations when the quote is a complete sentence: *The poet says in the first line, 'Today the world is a little more my own.'*

- Commas and full stops go outside the quotations when the quote is a phrase: *hit her like 'pots and pans'.*

- If you quote an entire line or more than one line, it should go on a separate line, without quotations, and indented. Like this:

  > *The words are muffled now, the laughing*
  > *Faces only a blur.*

6 Write your own examples of the three rules above using words, phrases and lines from the poem on page 90.

Guided writing

Write a response to the last two verses of the poem 'Punishment in Kindergarten' on page 90. Discuss the poet's contention that there's 'no need to remember'. Analyse the ideas and images, supporting your response with evidence from the poem, quoting words, phrases and/or lines.

Write your response to the last two verses of the poem.

Think/Plan

1 Read the whole poem again. Then work in pairs and discuss the following questions.

   a What memories does the poet evoke of that time?

   b What words and phrases does she use to evoke them?

   c What senses (sight, sound, smell, touch, taste) does the poet use to evoke the memories? Are they reliable?

   d Why does she say 'children are funny things'?

   e Why does she say there's 'no need to remember'? Do you think she really believes this?

> **Tip**
>
> When you write about a poem, you should read the poem carefully and look for ideas that are repeated or patterns in the poem.

2 Now decide on the main idea that you want to write about. The poet describes that 'honey-coloured day of peace'. Write a topic sentence about the memory that sets out what you are going to write about in more detail.

> **Useful language**
>
> **Phrases:** *The main point is…, The poet evokes…, In the first/second line…, The second/third verse…, The third line onwards…, For example,…, The use of the phrase…, The poem ends…*
>
> **Adverbs:** *mainly, obviously, particularly, especially, evidently, hopefully, briefly, consequently*
>
> **Reporting verbs:** *The poet/line/verse…, says, tells us, suggests, reveals, explains, claims, insists, discusses, wonders, asks*

Write: your comment

Write your first point about what the poet says about the memories. Write a topic sentence to introduce your main idea.

Start like this:

- The memory is still very vivid and painful because…

- The poet clearly believes that children can be cruel…

- The poet evokes the senses when she…

Write: continue your comment

Support your ideas with words and phrases quoted from the third verse of the poem.

- Explain what you think the poet is trying to express in each line or verse.

- Give examples of words and phrases to illustrate your points.

- Quote lines or groups of lines to support your ideas.

- Comment on or point out any ideas, words or phrases that are repeated and explain what you think they mean.

Write: finish the comment

Write your second point, again supporting your views with quotations from the final verse.

Think about these questions.

a How clear are the poet's memories?

b Do you think there's a contradiction between the 'beloved halts' and 'moving sadly on'?

c Do you think she has really found peace and that there's 'no need to remember'?

d What does the final image say to you?

e What is your general conclusion?

Things to remember when writing about poetry

- Read the poem carefully and look out for repeated themes or patterns.

- Explain the main subject matter of the poem – the story or themes.

- Explore the possible meanings and interpretations.

- Write a topic sentence to introduce your commentary.

- Organise your points clearly and support them with quotations.

- Show your knowledge by using the correct poetic terms and references.

- Demonstrate to the reader how you have engaged with the poem personally.

Check your first draft

When you have finished writing, be your own editor.

- Read your commentary of the poem and check that your points are clear and that you have quoted from the poem to support your ideas.

- Discuss your commentary with your partner and compare your ideas. Have you left out any important points?

Now write a second draft of your commentary on the poem.

Peer assessment

Before you give your work to your partner, tell him/her something that you'd like to improve about it so that he/she knows what to focus on.

Independent writing

Write a commentary of 350–400 words explaining your ideas about a poem.

Choose *one* of these ideas.

- A famous poem in your own language.

- A poem that you have studied at school.

- A song whose lyrics you find particularly interesting.

Write at least three paragraphs.

Follow these stages.

Stage 1 Generate ideas. Read the poem and discuss it with your partner. What is it about? Discuss the imagery.

Stage 2 Take notes on your ideas. Think of two or three points to make about the poem.

- What techniques and imagery does the poet use?

- What effect does this have on the reader?

- Which words and phrases can you quote to support your views?

Stage 3 Write your response to the poem, following your plan. Use the checklist to make sure your response is thoughtful.

Writer's checklist: critical responses

- Have you explained the main theme in the poem?

- Have you written a topic sentence setting out your main idea?

- Have you explored different interpretations of the subject matter?

- Have you supported your views with words, phrases and lines from the poem?

- Have you used the correct poetic terms?

- Have you demonstrated some personal engagement with the poem?

Editor's checklist

Check

- that your ideas are organised into paragraphs

- your spelling and use of capital letters

- punctuation – your use of quotation marks

- the grammar is correct – sentence adverbs.

Final draft

Once you have finished your commentary of the poem, print it out with a copy of the poem and post them on the classroom wall.

Check your progress

I can:	Needs more work	Almost there	All done!
write to analyse, review and comment			
explain the subject matter of a poem and explore different interpretations			
use evidence from the poem to support my views in the form of quotations			
use correct punctuation when writing quotations from the poem.			

10 Family journeys

Your writing aim for this unit: To write a story with a powerful description of place and people

Writing objectives for first language English	**Writing and Use of English objectives for second language English**
In this unit, you will:	In this unit, you will:
• learn a range of registers and a personal voice	• learn how to use participles
• use a wide variety of sentences for a range of purposes	• learn descriptive adjectives
• use a range of punctuation and different grammar choices to help with meaning and create a wide range of effects.	• use correct punctuation – commas.

Key terms that you will learn: mood   omniscient narrator   limited narrator

How can I write a vivid description in a story?

Effective descriptions in stories

A good description in a story should:

- provide a strong sense of *mood* and *atmosphere*
- focus on some or all of the *five senses*
- provide *vivid detail* about specific *items*, aspects of *nature* or *people*
- link *description* to the *characters*, *plot* or *action*.

Reading

It is important that you learn how to weave description into your stories. This will make them more atmospheric and striking. In this extract, a family get held up in a long queue of traffic. The father of the family goes to investigate, taking two of the children with him.

1 As you read the text, think about these questions:

  a What actually happens – if anything – in this story?

  b How vividly can you see, feel, hear, touch or taste the things the writer describes?

Five Hours to Simla

'Take me to see, Dadd-ee, take me to see,' the boys had begun to clamour, and to their astonishment he stood aside and let them climb out and even led them back to the truck that stood stalled imperviously across the culvert. The mother opened and shut her mouth silently. Her daughter stood up and hung over the front seat to watch their disappearing figures. In despair, she cried, 'They're gone!'

'Sit down! Where can they go?'

'I want to go too, Mumm-ee, I want to go too-oo.'

'Be quiet. There's nowhere to go.'

The girl began to wail. It was usually a good strategy in a family with loud voices but this time her sense of aggrievement was genuine: her head ached from the long sleep in the car, from the heat beating on its metal top, from the lack of air, from the glare and from hunger. 'I'm hung-ree,' she wept.

'We were going to eat when we reached Solan,' her mother reminded her. 'There's such a nice-nice restaurant at the railway station in Solan. Such nice-nice omelettes they make.'

'I want an omelette!' wailed the child.

'Wait till we get to Solan.'

'When will we reach it? When?'

'Oh, I don't know. Late. Sit down and open that basket at the back. You'll find something to eat there.'

But now that omelettes at Solan had been mentioned, the basket packed at home with Gluco biscuits and potato chips held no attraction for the girl. She stopped wailing but sulked instead, sucking her thumb, a habit she was supposed to have given up but which resurfaced for comfort when necessary.

She did not need to draw upon her thumb juices for long. The news of the traffic jam on the highway had spread like ripples from a stone thrown. From somewhere, it seemed from nowhere, for there was no village bazaar, marketplace or stalls visible in that dusty dereliction, wooden barrows came trundling along towards the waiting traffic, bearing freshly cut lengths of sugarcane and a machine to extract their juice into thick dirty grey glasses; bananas already more black than yellow from the sun that baked them, peanuts in their shells roasting in pans set on embers. Men, women and children were climbing over the ditch like phantoms, materialising out of the dust, with baskets on their heads filled not only with **sustenance** but with amusement as well – a tray load of paper toys painted indigo blue and violent pink. Small bamboo pipes that released rude noises and a dyed feather on a spool, both together. Kites, puppets, clay carts, wooden toys and tin whistles. The vendors milled around the buses, cars and rickshaws, and were soon standing at their car window, both vocally and manually proffering goods for sale.

The baby let drop the **narcotic** rubber nipple, delighted. His eyes grew big and shone at the flowering outside. The little girl was **perplexed**, wondering what to take from so much **abundance** till the perfect choice presented itself in a rainbow of colour: green, pink and violet – her favourites. It was a barrow of soft drinks, and nothing on this day of gritty dust, yellow sun and frustrating delay could be more enticing than those bottles filled with syrups in dazzling floral colours. She set up a scream of desire.

'Are you mad?' her mother said promptly. 'You think I'll let you drink a bottle full of **typhoid and cholera** germs?'

The girl gasped with disbelief at being denied. Her mouth opened wide to issue a protest but her mother went on, 'After you have your typhoid-and-cholera injection you may. You want a nice big typhoid-and-cholera injection first?'

The child's mouth was still open in contemplation of the impossible choice when her brothers came plodding back through the dust, each carrying a **pith** and bamboo toy – a clown that bounced up and down on a stick and a bird that whirled upon a pin. Behind them the father slouched **morosely**. He had his hands deep in his pockets and his face was lined with a frown deeply embedded with dust.

'We'll be here for hours,' he informed his wife through the car window.

From 'Five Hours to Simla' by Anita Desai

How the text works

Do you remember what makes a good description in a story? Here is how the writer makes it work. She:

- focuses on the details of the experience: the children, the heat, the vendors, etc.
- uses expanded noun phrases (for example, 'freshly cut lengths of sugarcane') or long sentences to describe aspects of the setting
- evokes the **mood** through the use of well-chosen imagery
- moves skilfully between the different registers of the speakers.

Key term

mood: the general feeling that the atmosphere and tone create in the reader

Text analysis

1 Nothing dramatic happens in the extract, but there *is* development.

   a What happens right at the start of the extract, and how does it change the mood in the car?

   b How does that mood change again when the sellers appear?

Reading closely

2 Desai describes in detail two main elements in the extract: the daughter and her reactions, and the appearance of the sellers.

   a What does the daughter do in the first paragraph when the father gets out with the boys?

   b What has made her head ache, according to what we are told in the second paragraph?

3 Good description often includes specific rather than general ideas or nouns (for example, 'apples' and 'apricots' rather than 'fruit').

   a What specific items of food do the vendors suddenly appear carrying?

   b What items for 'amusement' do the vendors also bring?

   c What particular item does the daughter decide she wants?

4 The writer also uses two powerful images to describe the vendors' activities. Can you identify the two similes in the following sentences? Write a sentence explaining what they tell the reader.

   a 'The news of the traffic jam on the highway had spread like ripples from a stone thrown.'

   b 'Men, women and children were climbing over the ditch like phantoms, materialising out of the dust...'

5 Another important element in the description is the use of a different register for the daughter from the mother.

   a Identify at least two examples where the daughter repeats words or phrases in her reactions to what her mother says.

   b What does this tell us about the child's state of mind?

6 Can you identify any other ways in which Desai conveys the idea that this is a child talking?

Thinking about the text

The world as the mother and daughter – and the baby – see it is evoked very well by the writer.

7 Think carefully and then answer these questions.

a What does the sentence 'The mother opened and shut her mouth silently' suggest about what she feels when her husband leaves the car with the boys?

b Why do you think the daughter is not satisfied with the mother's offer of the basket of snacks they have in the car?

c What impression do you get of the mother from the passage (think in particular about the last section when the daughter asks for a drink)?

> cruel   protective   tired
>
> fed-up   happy   grumpy

d There are a number of different types of narrator writers can use in stories. Two of these are **limited** and **omniscient**.

- What sort of narrator is Desai using here? Is it one style more than the other?

- What evidence do you have for this?

- What effect does this have in a story like this? (Does the reader know more than the characters, or the same?)

Key terms

omniscient narrator: a narrator who is all-seeing – they can jump in time and place, letting the reader know about people and actions which the characters in the story might not be able to see.

limited narrator: this is often when a story is told through a particular character's eyes. They have a limited knowledge of what is happening – they cannot see beyond their own experience.

React to the text

8 Work in pairs. Discuss these questions.

a In the story, the family is stuck in a traffic jam with no prospect, it seems, of it ending. Have you ever been stuck in a large traffic jam with your own family? How did you feel? What was the setting – was it in a city?

b How effective do you think the passage is in conveying the setting and the feelings of the family? Copy and complete the grid below with evidence from the text.

Features	Evidence
Use of some/all of the senses	
Precise vocabulary	
Vivid imagery	
Extended descriptive phrases	
A range of different details described	
Sense of the mood or atmosphere	
Strong sense of character or people	

Use of English

Later in the unit you will write a description of a journey.

Participles

Grammar presentation

The *–ing* form in English is very flexible. As well as indicating continuous forms (*I am eating*), the *–ing* form can be used as an adjective, adverb or in clauses. The past participle can also be used in the same ways. These forms are called participles and they are very useful in descriptive language.

1 Look at the following phrases from the text on pages 100–101. Match the *–ing* forms to their uses.

   a to watch their *disappearing* figures

   b wooden barrows came *trundling* along

   c peanuts in their shells *roasting* in pans set on embers

   i adverb

   ii participle clause

   iii adjective

2 Find more examples of the three different uses of *–ing* forms in the text.

Note: An adverb tells you how something was done, for example how the wooden barrows came.

A participle clause replaces a relative clause, for example peanuts...which were roasting.

Now look at these sentences from the text on pages 100–101. The past participles are used to identify the noun, just as in a relative clause.

- the basket *packed* at home with Gluco biscuits (the basket that had been packed)

- bottles *filled* with syrups (the bottles that were filled with syrups)

But sometimes they are used before nouns like an adjective:

- a *dyed* feather on a spool

3 Decide if the *–ing* forms in these sentences are adjectives, adverbs or participle clauses.

   a The little boy stood there considering what to do next.

   b Amin lay in bed listening to the falling rain.

   c The car coming up the hill belonged to the doctor.

   d Esma wondered who the man talking to her mother was.

   e She listened to the creaking sound coming from behind the door.

4 Choose the correct option to complete each sentence.

   a Vania ate her sandwich and listened to the *howling / howled* winds outside.

   b The men carried huge bags *filling / filled* with clothes.

   c The freshly *painting / painted* door had been left open.

   d We sat in the *baking / baked* sun, *waiting / waited* for the bus.

Vocabulary: descriptive adjectives

Vocabulary presentation

In descriptions, writers often use adjectives to describe the shape, size, condition, colour, material, etc. of an object to give the reader a clearer picture of it.

5 Circle the adjectives in each of these phrases from the text on pages 100–101 and say what aspect of the objects they describe.

a thick dirty grey glasses

b paper toys painted indigo blue and violent pink

c clay carts, wooden toys and tin whistles

6 Descriptive adjectives in English go in a particular order before nouns.

a / the	
Opinion	beautiful
Size	small
Age	antique
Shape	round
Colour	red
Origin	Chinese
Material	wooden
box	

Look at the order of adjectives in these noun phrases. Tick (✓) the correct ones and correct the ones that are in the wrong order.

a a small, bright pink canvas bag

b a green, old woollen sweater

c an ugly, modern, tall glass building

d a massive, square, old, golden frame

e her favourite, blue, Italian leather shoes

7 Describe some of the objects in this room.

a small, old-fashioned, brown leather suitcase

Tip

Note that we never include adjectives from all the types in a description because it's too complicated. Three or four adjectives are usually enough.

Punctuation: commas

Punctuation presentation

In direct speech, we use commas before and after the name of the person who is being addressed.

'Take me to see, Dadd-ee, take me to see,'…

8 Insert commas in the correct place(s) in each sentence.

a 'Where are you going Qiongzhi?'

b 'Hello Mr Khatri welcome back.'

c 'Can I go with you Uncle Vihaan?'

d 'Sit down Susannah and finish your dinner.'

e So Fahad where have you been?'

Guided writing

The family in the description on pages 100–101 continue their journey. But an hour later, their old car overheats and breaks down. They are now stuck in the middle of the countryside by a river. Include dialogue and mix in some action – for example, the father finds a shepherd minding a flock of goats who is willing to help them, or they decide to spend the night in an old hut they find nearby.

Write a description of the place where they stop.

Think/Plan

1 Work in pairs. Generate ideas for your description. Answer the questions to help you.

   a Where does the car break down? Describe the place.

   b What is the reaction of the different members of the family?

   c What does the shepherd look like?

   d What does the hut look like?

   e What other details can you include in your description?

Tip

When writing a description, it helps to picture the place, objects, etc. You can look at photos to help you get ideas.

2 Plan your description. The extract on pages 100–101 starts with a short exchange between the characters mixed in with some description, then focuses more on description, before ending with some more dialogue.

Useful language

Speech verbs: *cried, clamoured, wailed, wept, reminded him/her/them, said, told him/her/them, went on, informed, admitted, suggested, asked, whispered*

Participles: *the smoking engine, the blistering heat, the river flowing nearby, some birds flying overhead, a shepherd standing on a hill, the mountains covered in snow*

Descriptive adjectives: Colours: *violet, indigo, turquoise, bright red, dark grey, violent pink;* **Materials:** *leather, clay, tin, paper, wooden, plastic, glass;* **Condition:** *dirty, cracked, torn, twisted, bent, stained, shiny, chipped*

Write: start your description

Write the first part of your description.

Think about the opening lines of your description. How are you going to start? Here are two ideas.

- Describe the old car the family are travelling in and what's happened to it.
- Start with a short dialogue between some members of the family.

Write: focus on description

Write a longer paragraph or two short paragraphs of description.

Here are some ideas for things you can describe:

- the surroundings where the car has broken down: trees, mountains, river, sounds, smells, etc.
- introduce a person or a group of people who arrive on the scene, and describe them
- the mother decides to break out the packed lunch – describe the different types of food, containers, etc.

Write: finish the description

Now write the end of your description. A solution is found for the broken-down car. Say what this is and write a short dialogue between members of the family.

Here are some ideas.

- A shepherd/goatherd has offered to lead them to a nearby village.
- The family decide to stay in the car and sleep in it overnight.
- The father sets out on his own to seek help.

Things to remember when writing a description

- Use a mixture of dialogue and description to keep the reader's interest.
- Provide details about the surroundings, aspects of nature and people and specific items.
- Use a variety of sentence structures, types and lengths: longer for the descriptions and shorter for the dialogue.
- Use extended noun phrases with participles and descriptive adjectives.
- Use past tenses throughout your description.

Check your first draft

When you have finished writing, be your own editor.

- Take a step back from your work. When you have finished, take a break, then come back to it.
- Read your description from a reader's perspective and try to be critical.
- Look out for words or phrases that you have repeated and try to change them.

Now write a second draft of your description.

Peer assessment

Remember to tell your partner where you think they have been successful in their description before you tell them where they can improve.

Independent writing

Write a description of 350–400 words.
Choose *one* of these ideas or use your own.

- Flight delayed – stuck in the airport waiting lounge.
- On a school trip, the bus breaks down on a mountainside.
- Going home on an underground railway, the train breaks down in a tunnel.

Write using paragraphs and blend the description with dialogue.

Follow these stages.

Stage 1 Generate ideas. Imagine the situation: the surroundings, other people, and possible dialogues.

Stage 2 Put your ideas into a plan. Take notes with your ideas for the description and dialogue.

- How will you start your description?
- What are you going to describe?
- What happens in the end?

Stage 3 Write your description in paragraphs, following your plan. Use the checklist to make sure your description is interesting.

Check your progress

I can:	Needs more work	Almost there	All done!
use a wide range of registers and personal voice			
demonstrate control of a wide range of different structures for effect and purpose			
use grammar and punctuation to enhance meaning and create different effects			
evoke mood and atmosphere through description and dialogue.			

11 Explaining events

Your writing aim for this unit: To write an article about an aspect of a different culture

Writing objectives for first language English	**Writing and Use of English objectives for second language English**
In this unit, you will:	In this unit, you will:
• select from a wide and varied vocabulary for a range of tasks, purposes and readers	• use a variety of subordinate clauses
• use a range of formal and informal styles to create meaning and a wide range of effects	• learn vocabulary related to festivals
• use a range of punctuation and different grammar choices to help with meaning and create a wide range of effects.	• use cohesion – examples and emphasis.

Key terms that you will learn: subheading   colon   subordinate clause   main clause

How can I write an informative article about a different country or culture?

There are lots of famous festivals around the world, and your own country will have its special days or celebrations. Which of the following have you heard of? (You may need to do some quick research.)

- The Rio Carnival, Brazil
- Holi, festival of colour, India
- The Notting Hill Carnival, London, United Kingdom
- The Lantern festival, China

Add any other famous national festivals you know. Talk with a friend/partner about which of these you would most like to attend. Why?

Effective explanatory articles

A good explanatory article should:

- provide *clear information* in a *structured way*
- contain a *mix* of relevant *facts* and *individual* or more *personal details*
- have a *main theme* or *core idea* that holds the information together
- maintain a *balanced, informative tone* appropriate to the audience
- use a headline and **subheadings** (where needed).

> ### Key term
>
> **subheading**: heading for a section of text that goes beneath the main headline

Reading

Magazines and newspapers often try to interest readers in events or experiences outside their own lives. The following article comes from a travel website's page called 'The World's Great Festivals'.

1 As you read the text, think about these questions:

a What is the core idea about the festival that runs through the article?

b How does the article make the reader interested in the festival?

The World's Great Festivals

No. 3 The Day of the Dead, Mexico

Why the Day of the Dead is really all about life.

This festival makes our top ten because it is unique, heart-warming and not quite what it seems.

The Spectre Effect

Anyone who has seen the opening shots of the 2015 James Bond film *Spectre* will know all about the Day of the Dead. It shows a huge carnival procession moving through the streets of Mexico City, with participants dressed in full-length skeleton costumes or as giant **marionettes**, alongside enormous decorated floats. The faces and figures are frightening and (unsurprisingly for a James Bond film) death and danger are never far away.

But the reality is somewhat different. Mexico City had never had a 'Day of the Dead' festival like this when the film was made, although following the success of the film the government decided to introduce one in 2016. You may be surprised to know that the Day of the Dead is traditionally a private, smaller affair that takes place in people's homes or at candlelit ceremonies in cemeteries. Not so good for a **Hollywood blockbuster**, but interesting for other reasons.

What is its purpose?

Although people may choose to observe the day in different ways, all are celebrating the lives of the departed. **Celebrants** believe that on the chosen day the spirits of their loved ones return. So, the living need to be ready and waiting. Families build altars displaying items the deceased liked while alive, including particular foods or drinks. There are photographs of the dead too, and **votive candles** to light their return. All share a sincere belief: there is an everlasting connection between the dead and their families. Those who object to larger community events think that big parades or festivals will damage that belief, and make the celebrations much less personal.

How did it all begin?

So, what is the history of the Day of the Dead, or *Dia de Muertos*, to give it its Spanish name? Is it just another version

---

Glossary

spectre: ghost or phantom

marionette: puppet, usually controlled with strings

Hollywood blockbuster: big-budget American film

celebrants: people who follow or take part in the festival

votive candles: small candles burned in offering or prayer

of the Halloween festival? Originally, it was probably an Aztec festival dedicated to the goddess Mictecacihuatl, and took place at the beginning of the summer. However, after the Spanish took control of Mexico in the 16th century it gradually became associated with 31 October, 1 and 2 November – so as to coincide with Christian celebrations around All Saints' Eve, All Saints' Day and All Souls' Day. But it wasn't until the 21st century that the Mexican government created a national holiday. The Day of the Dead itself is now celebrated on 2 November.

What makes it so special?

There are many things that make the celebration memorable. The bright marigold flowers that adorn the altars are thought to attract the souls of the dead to the offerings laid out for them. Some even believe the strong scent of the flowers guides souls from the cemeteries to their family homes. Pillows and blankets are often left out too, so that the dead can 'rest' after their lengthy journey back to the world of the living. Families also hold picnics and small parties to celebrate the memories of the dead, telling stories about them or dancing to honour their memory.

Why is the skull so important?

Perhaps most striking is the image of the skull, which is everywhere. In particular, you will see people adopting the popular design of an attractive, well-dressed woman with a skeleton face, known as La Calavera Catrina, and inspired by an artwork of that name – a contradictory symbol of the Day of the Dead festivities. In fact, masks that look like skulls are everywhere. There are even delicious skulls made of chocolate or sugar that are given both to the living and the dead. What is clear is that remembering the dead does not have to be a solemn, depressing event but a tender, often joyful memorial.

What if you can't get to Mexico?

While most people associate the Day of the Dead with Mexico, similar festivities take place all over Central and South America, from Bolivia to Brazil, and in other parts of the world, particularly those with large Mexican communities, such as the United States. It seems like the dead are here to stay!

How the text works

Do you remember what makes a good informative article? Here is how the writer makes it work. He/She:

- uses organisational features (for example, subheadings) to divide the information effectively

- uses present tense forms to explain the present situation, and past tense forms to fill in background and history

- has a formal style, but uses a variety of sentence types and lengths to keep the text lively and interesting

- provides visual details that create a full picture of the event (for example, 'giant marionettes').

Text analysis

1 The main purpose of the article is to explain. But it is not a news report: these tend to be about specific, newsworthy events that have just happened. So, what exactly does this article explain? Write a sentence summing it up. You could use this structure:

This article explains what _____
and how _____ .

Reading closely

2 The order of the article is important: what does each section focus on? Work in a small group to discuss each question below and agree your response. Use the subheadings in the article to help you.

a Which film does the opening paragraph mention? Why?

b How is the way of celebrating mentioned in the second paragraph different from that shown in the film?

c The third paragraph talks about the origins of the festival: why do you think the writer chose not to begin with this?

d What explanations are given in the fifth paragraph for including marigolds and pillows and blankets in some memorials?

e What evidence is given in the sixth paragraph to support the idea that skulls and skeletons give happiness and reflect beauty?

f The last paragraph ends with a sort of joke that sums up the article as a whole. What is the 'joke' and why is it a good way to end?

3 The explanatory tone of the article is created in a number of ways. One of these is through connectives that help to explain the origins of the festival. Look again at the fourth paragraph.

So, what is the history of the Day of the Dead, or *Dia de Muertos*, to give it its Spanish name? Is it just another version of the Halloween festival? <u>Originally</u>, it was probably an Aztec festival dedicated to the goddess Mictecacihuatl, and took place <u>at the beginning</u> of the summer. <u>However</u>, <u>after</u> the Spanish took control of Mexico in the 16th century it gradually became associated with 31 October, 1 and 2 November – so as to coincide with Christian celebrations around All Saints' Eve, All Saints' Day and All Souls' Day. But it wasn't until the 21st century that the Mexican government created a national holiday. The Day of the Dead itself is <u>now</u> celebrated on 2 November.

Can you replace the underlined connectives with words from the box below?

at present	but	when
initially		at the start

4 There are three uses of punctuation (apart from the usual full stops, exclamations and question marks) that help the explanation. Identify one example:

a of brackets used for additional information

b of a **colon** used to introduce an explanatory clause

c of a comma used in the second paragraph to divide a **subordinate clause** and a **main clause**?

> ### Key terms
>
> **colon**: the symbol : used to introduce items in a list or an explanation
>
> **subordinate clause**: a clause that is dependent on the main clause to make sense. It often begins with a conjunction (<u>I liked him</u> (main clause), <u>even though</u> (conjunction) <u>he beat me at tennis</u> (subordinate clause)).
>
> **main clause**: a clause that can stand alone and make sense without any further information, such as a sentence

Thinking about the text

5 Think carefully and then answer these questions.

a The writer says La Calavera Catrina is a 'contradictory symbol'. What is contradictory about it? (Think about the woman's appearance.)

b Based on the sixth paragraph, what do you think the writer of the article thinks about how families remember the dead in Mexico?

React to the text

6 Work in pairs. Discuss these questions.

a Is the Day of the Dead similar to any festivities in your own culture? If so, what?

b How would you feel if this was a normal family celebration in your family? Would you 'like' it?

c Do you think readers would be drawn to visit a Day of the Dead celebration based on this article? Why/why not?

Use of English

Later in the unit you will write about another famous festival.

Subordinate clauses

Grammar presentation

In most types of text, but especially in informative writing, writers use longer sentences with subordinate clauses in them. These clauses depend on the main clause and cannot stand alone.

1 Look at the following sentences from the article on pages 110–111. What is the main clause? What is the subordinate clause?

   a Mexico City had never had a 'Day of the Dead' festival like this when the film was made, although following the success of the film the government decided to introduce one in 2016.

   b Pillows and blankets are often left out too, so that the dead can 'rest' after their lengthy journey back to the world of the living.

2 Which of the subordinate clauses above:

   a expresses purpose?

   b contrasts with the main clause?

3 Copy the table and complete it with the connectives used to indicate subordinate clauses according to their meaning.

| so as to | though |
| because | therefore | despite |
| so that |

Purpose	
Contrast	
Cause/effect	

Can you add two more connectives to each type?

4 Match the parts of the sentences. What type of subordinate clause is used in each one?

a Although the Carnival in Rio de Janeiro is the biggest carnival in the world

b The Sambodromo in Rio de Janeiro was specially constructed

c The mayor of Rio hands over the keys of the city to King Momo

d King Momo takes the city keys

e You'd better like samba music

i as he is said to be the king of the Carnival celebrations.

ii so as to show that the Carnival can begin.

iii similar celebrations are held in many other Brazilian cities.

iv because it's almost the only music you'll hear!

v so that people could see the Carnival parade.

Vocabulary: festivals

5 Circle the words related to festivals in this sentence from the article on page 110–111.

It shows a huge carnival procession moving through the streets of Mexico City, with participants dressed in full-length skeleton costumes or as giant marionettes, alongside enormous decorated floats.

Find at least ten more words related to festivals and celebrations in the article.

6 Complete the paragraph below using the words in the box.

> celebrations   floats   festivities
>
> parties   hold   take place
>
> parades   costumes
>
> band   participants

In the Sambodromo, the samba schools
(a) _____ massive
(b) _____. All the **(c)** _____
line up, wearing elaborate
(d) _____ and they dance and
play instruments, accompanied by
massive, colourful **(e)** _____.
Although the Sambodromo is the centre
of the Carnival **(f)** _____, smaller
(g) _____ called 'blocos'
(h) _____ in the streets all around
the city. People dance to the sounds of a
samba **(i)** _____ and the
(j) _____ can go on for hours.

Cohesion: examples and emphasis

7 Look at these sentences from the article on pages 110–111. Write the missing preposition for each one.

a _____ particular, you will see people adopting the popular design of an attractive, well-dressed woman with a skeleton face…

b _____ fact, masks that look like skulls are everywhere.

8 Complete the following example and emphasis connectives with the missing words.

a _____ example

b _____ this case

c _____ this in mind

d _____ an illustration

e such _____

f _____ instance

Guided writing

The Carnival (or *Carnaval*) in Rio de Janeiro, Brazil is, according to the *Guinness World Records*, the biggest party in the world. A travel website has commissioned you to write an article about the Rio Carnival. Include the following information: popular misconceptions and the reality; the purpose of the Carnival; the historical background; some specific details and features; other similar carnivals.

Write an article for a travel website.

Think/Plan

1 Work in pairs. Generate ideas for your articles. Answer the questions to help you.

  a What do you know about the Carnival in Rio?

  b When is it celebrated?

  c Why do people celebrate Carnival?

  d Where does it come from?

  e Where else is Carnival celebrated?

2 Now do some research into the Carnival in Rio and take notes.

Tip

In researching a topic, it helps to write down questions or key words. You can then use these questions/keywords to structure your article.

Useful language

Phrases: *Anyone who has...will know all about..., Have you ever...?, Can you imagine?, In reality..., So what is the history of...?, The celebrations date back to..., It was first celebrated..., What is clear is that..., Perhaps most striking is the image of..., Similar festivities take place all over..., It seems like...*

Connectives for clauses: *so as to, so that, to, in order to, though, despite, although, after, until, before, when, if, in case, provided, because, therefore, so, in fact, in particular, for example, such as, for instance, as an illustration, in this case, with this in mind*

Festivals: *adorn, altar, band, carnival, celebrations, ceremony, costumes, event, festivities, floats, hold, memorial, marionettes, national holiday, parades, participants, parties, picnic, take place*

Write: the opening

The opening paragraph of an article often tries to pull the readers into the topic by addressing them directly or using a reference to an idea (often a misconception) people have about something.

Write the first paragraph of your article. Try to attract the reader using one (or some) of these techniques.

Present a popular misconception about the topic, and then the reality or truth.

- Anyone who has seen TV footage of the Carnival will believe that...

- It is commonly believed that Rio's Carnival is...

- But in fact,...

- However, the reality is...

Ask a rhetorical question.

- Can you imagine being in Rio...?

- What would you do if...?

Write: factual information

Using the notes from your research, write a paragraph about each of the following topics.

a Beliefs or theories about the purpose or reasons people celebrate Carnival.

b Some of the historical background of the celebrations.

Write: details

Now turn the focus of the article on a particular aspect of Carnival. It could be something that is less well-known about the celebrations.

Here are some ideas:

- special food or dishes that are eaten in Carnival

- 'blocos' – smaller street parties that are held around the city

- Carnival as a tourist attraction for the cities where it is celebrated

- how samba schools prepare for Carnival

- the musical and percussion instruments used in samba music.

Write: finish your article

Write about other places where Carnival is celebrated in a similar way.

Here are some ideas:

- New Orleans, USA

- Notting Hill, UK

- Mazatlan, Mexico

- Venice, Italy

- Goa, India.

Things to remember when writing about an event

- Provide clear information about the topic in a structured way.

- Include a mix of facts and more personal details.

- Build your article around a core idea that holds the information together.

- Use a headline and subheadings for each section of your article.

- Use present tenses to describe the celebrations and past tenses to explain the background.

- Use a variety of sentence types, with different types of subordinate clause to maintain the reader's interest.

- Use connectives to join your ideas within and between paragraphs.

- Employ the correct words and phrases to describe a festivity.

Check your first draft

When you have finished writing, be your own editor.

- Work in pairs. Use your article as notes to make an oral presentation to your partner about the Rio Carnival and the particular aspect of it that you have focused on.

- Then give your article to your partner to read.

- Read your partner's article and discuss whether they have managed to keep your interest and if they have successfully mixed factual information with a more personal viewpoint.

Peer assessment

Before you start, work with your partner and write three things that you think make a good travel article. Then review each other's work on those criteria.

Now write a second draft of your article.

Independent writing

Write an article of 350–400 words about a particular aspect of a different culture.

Choose *one* of these ideas or use your own.

- New Year
- Halloween
- A very well-known festival in another country

Write at least three to four paragraphs.

Follow these stages.

Stage 1 Generate ideas. Think about what you already know about the topic. Do some research into other aspects of the topic: common misconceptions; purpose and background; specific details; similar events in other places.

Stage 2 Put your ideas into a plan, using your research questions to structure your notes.

- What do people commonly associate with the celebration? What is the reality?
- What is the historical background?
- What particular aspect would you like to focus on?

Stage 3 Write your article in paragraphs, following your plan. Use the checklist to make sure your article is both informative and interesting.

Writer's checklist: articles

- Have you provided information in a clear and structured way?
- Have you blended information and more specific details?
- Have you found a core idea that holds all of your information together?
- Have you used different sentence types, some with subordinate clauses with different functions?
- Have you used appropriate vocabulary to describe different aspects of the celebrations?
- Have you included a headline and used a subheading before each section?

Editor's checklist

Check

- that your ideas are organised into paragraphs
- your spelling and use of capital letters
- punctuation, especially commas
- the grammar is correct – subordinate clauses.

Final draft

Once you have finished your article, collect the class's work together and publish the articles as a magazine.

Check your progress

I can:	Needs more work	Almost there	All done!
provide clear information in a structured way			
use both formal and less formal styles to enhance and emphasise meaning and create different effects			
use organisational features to divide information effectively			
make my writing more interesting by providing visual details and giving a full picture of the event.			

12 Finding freedom

Your writing aim for this unit: To write a powerful story about someone on their own	
Writing objectives for first language English In this unit, you will: • create and sustain character, viewpoint and voice • use a wide variety of sentences for a range of purposes • shape and craft sentences so they add to the overall development of the text.	**Writing and Use of English objectives for second language English** In this unit, you will: • use active and passive continuous forms • learn words related to nature • use cohesion – connectives for narratives.
Key terms that you will learn: protagonist phrasal verb	

How do I write a story with an atmospheric setting and a strong protagonist?

This unit is all about you generating ideas for a story which has atmosphere and a strong main character. Look at the image on page 119. Using it as a stimulus for discussion, work with a partner to generate ideas explaining what is going on: who is the person? Where are they? What has just happened? How do you think he feels? You might end up reusing these ideas later, so keep a note of them.

Effective third person narratives

A good third person narrative should:

- *interest* the reader in the *main character* or **protagonist**

- create *obstacles* or *problems* he or she must *overcome*

- create a *strong sense of voice*

- link *setting, situation or experiences* to the main *storyline*

- use *dialogue*, where needed, to reveal or develop *the plot* or *characterisation*.

> **Key term**
>
> **protagonist**: the main character in a story

Reading

Mehmed, My Hawk tells the story of a poor village boy who runs away from the local tribal leader, Abdi Agha – 'old Goat-beard'. In this extract, Mehmed has fled to find another village where someone might employ him.

1 As you read the text, think about these questions:

  a How does the writer create a vivid sense of the setting?

  b What questions are raised in your mind as you read it?

The Escape

The boy running through the thistles was panting. He had been running now for a long time without a stop. All at once he halted. Blood was oozing from where the thistles had scratched him. He could hardly stand. He was scared. Would he escape? Fearfully he looked over his shoulder. There was no one in sight. He felt more hopeful, turned to the right and ran for a while. Then he was so tired that he lay down to rest among the thistles. On his left he saw an ant-heap. The ants were big and the entrance to their nest was **teeming** with activity. For a while he forgot everything as he watched them. Then, pulling himself together, he rose suddenly from the ground and resumed his flight to the right. Soon he emerged from the thistles and sank to his knees. Seeing that his head still showed above the thistles, he crouched on his **haunches**. He began to rub his bleeding legs with earth. He could feel the sting as it touched them.

The rocks were only a little farther. With all his remaining strength he started to run towards them and soon reached the plane-tree below the tallest. At the foot of the tree he found a deep hollow like a well, filled with yellow, golden and red-veined leaves piled high, reaching half-way up the trunk. The dry leaves rustled as he threw himself down on them. On the tip of one bare branch of the tree a bird was perched, but it flew off, scared by the noise. The boy was tired and would have liked to spend the night there. But it occurred to him that this was impossible: the wilds were full of man-eating wolves and birds of prey. Some of the leaves still hanging from the tree floated down to join the others. One at a time they began to fall on his body. He talked to himself, quite loud, as if someone were beside him.

'I'll go,' he said. 'I'll go and find that village. No one knows about my going there. I won't turn back. I'll be a goatherd. Let my mother look for me. Let her search as long as she likes. Old Goat-beard will never see my face again. If I cannot find that village, I'll die of hunger. I'll die, and that's the end of it.'

The autumn sun was warm. It **caressed** the rocks, the plane-tree, the leaves. The soil was fresh in the sunlight. A few autumn flowers were already beginning to appear. The **asphodel** had a bitter scent and glistened with moisture. In autumn the mountains smell of asphodel.

Had he been there one hour or two? He wasn't sure. But the sun had sunk behind the mountain ridge. Some

time later the boy stopped muttering to himself and suddenly remembered he was being pursued. He became **frantic**. He had forgotten to watch the sun, which had set without his noticing it. Where must he go now, in which direction? A faint goat-track meandered among the rocks. He began to follow it. He ran without heeding the rocks, the bushes and the stones. His weariness had passed. He stopped, looked around for a moment, then ran again.

His feet pounded the soil. As he ran a tiny lizard on a rotten tree-stump caught his eye. The boy felt glad for some reason, but aware of being watched, the lizard disappeared beneath the tree.

The boy stumbled and stopped. He felt dizzy and black spots were dancing before his eyes. The earth seemed to spin around him like a top. His hands and legs were trembling. After looking back a moment he began to run again. Once a flight of **partridges** rose suddenly nearby and startled him. Any sound scared him and his heart was beating very fast. Hopelessly he glanced back again, drenched in sweat. His knee gave way beneath him and he sank to the ground on a small stony slope. He could smell his own **acrid** sweat, but mingled with the pleasant scent of flowers. Though he could hardly open his eyes, he raised his head heavily, fearfully, and looked below, where he could barely **distinguish** a mud roof. His joy was so great that his heart seemed to leap up into his mouth. Smoke curled slowly from the chimney, twisting this way and that, not black but a light purple. Behind him he heard a sound, as of footsteps, and he looked back fearfully. To the left the forest was like a black curtain of rain between sky and earth threatening to **engulf** him. He started to talk, no longer muttering now but shouting aloud as he ran away from the forest.

From *Mehmed, My Hawk* by Yasar Kemal

Key language features

continuous tenses

nature vocabulary

connectives

Glossary

teeming: containing large numbers of people or animals

haunches: the top of a person's legs and bottom

caressed: stroked gently

asphodel: a type of flower with small white petals

frantic: panicky

partridge: a brown, grey and white bird

acrid: strong, bitter smell

distinguish: see what something is

engulf: cover completely

How the text works

Do you remember what makes a good opening to a narrative? Here is how the writer makes it work. He:

- makes the reader curious by withholding information

- gives his protagonist a strong narrative voice, for example, in dialogue ('I'll die')

- has action that builds up more and more tension as the protagonist tries to escape

- describes the world around the main character using a varied vocabulary.

Text analysis

1 Although this extract is from the second chapter, it is where the story really gets going. Why does it work so well as an opening? Jot down your ideas and then share them with a partner.

Reading closely

2 Writers often use 'rise and fall' to keep the reader interested. This could mean the protagonist faces increasing danger, then the tension drops as he or she reaches temporary safety. Does this passage work in the same way?

Rate each of the following moments from the story on a scale of 1 (not very tense) to 10 (very tense or dramatic).

- Beginning of the story up to 'Would he escape?'

- Lying watching the ant-heap

- Sleeping in the hollow of the plane-tree

- Waking up – 'suddenly he remembered he was being pursued'

- Realising he'd forgotten to watch the sun

- Seeing the 'tiny lizard'

- His knee giving way, and him sinking down on the stony ground

- Seeing the house with the chimney/ smoke

- Hearing a sound behind him

- Running away from the forest

3 Now share your ideas with others – and justify why you have given such a score to each moment. What evidence is there from the language?

4 A range of factors make the opening effective. Working in groups of three, each of you should take *one* of the aspects from the diagram below and add your own notes on what we find out.

For each one, try to find five quotations from the extract that tell us about these aspects. Some quotations may cover all these aspects in one go.

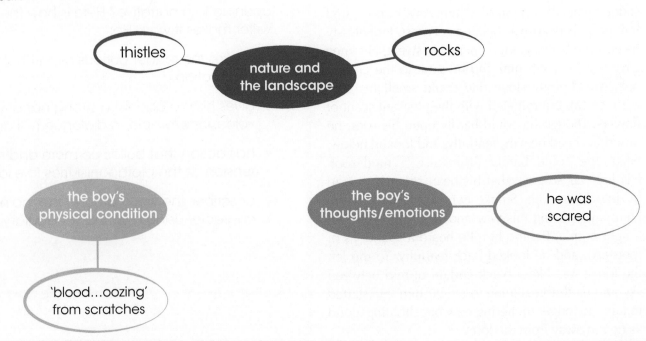

5 You have already identified a lot of the language used in the passage, but a core element is the fact that the boy is on the run. Therefore, there are lots of verbs of movement in the passage.

a In the first paragraph, what verb means to 'come out from inside'?

b In the second paragraph, what **phrasal verb** means 'made himself fall suddenly'?

c In the fifth paragraph, what verb tells us that someone was trying to 'catch up' with the boy?

d In the seventh paragraph, what verb means to trip up or lose your footing?

e In the seventh paragraph, what verb describes how the boy was 'shaking'?

> **Key term**
>
> **phrasal verb**: main verb with an adverb or preposition ('look out', 'look up', etc.)

Thinking about the text

Although the extract seems straightforward, there are some surprising details.

6 Think carefully and then answer these questions.

a What does the boy say about his mother? What is surprising about this?

b What do you think has happened to him to make him run away?

c How would you describe the character of the boy in the story? Consider these adjectives and decide which you think are most accurate.

- foolish
- brave
- determined
- frightened
- exhausted
- idiotic
- cunning

React to the text

7 Work in pairs. Discuss these questions.

a In the story, the boy has to find his way by the sun. Have you ever had to navigate your way to a place without a map, mobile phone or other guidance? How did you do it? Did you succeed or get lost?

b How would you feel if you were in the same situation as the boy?

c In what ways do you think the extract is effective as an opening to a story? Think about:

- the ways in which it raises questions
- how it makes us sympathetic to the main character
- how it uses tension and suspense.

Use of English

Later in the unit you will write part of a story.

Continuous tenses: active and passive

Grammar presentation

1 Look at the following sentences from the story on pages 120–121. Underline the verbs with continuous aspect. Which one is passive? What type of action do they describe?

a He had been running now for a long time without a stop.

b …the entrance to their nest was teeming with activity.

c …the boy stopped muttering to himself and suddenly remembered he was being pursued.

2 Match the continuous forms to the names of the tenses.

a am/is/are running	**i** past continuous passive
b was/were running	**ii** present continuous passive
c had been running	**iii** present continuous
d am/is/are being followed	**iv** past perfect continuous
e was/were being followed	**v** past perfect continuous passive*
f had been being followed	**vi** past continuous

*Note that this tense is not very common in English.

In stories, the 'narrative tenses', i.e. past tenses, are more common.

3 Choose the correct form to complete each sentence.

a She *had been following / had been being followed* the river for an hour when she found a small hut.

b Ahmed felt like he *was watching / was being watched*.

c He couldn't run very fast because he *was wearing / was being worn* sandals.

d The small house *was repairing / was being repaired* because there were piles of brick and cement.

e Hira *had been walking / had been being walked* since early morning and now she was exhausted.

4 Complete this extract from the story with the correct continuous form of the verbs in brackets.

The evening sun **(a)** _____ (go) down on the horizon, and Rafi **(b)** _____ (limp) for an hour. His ankle was very swollen. They knew it was time to stop.

Rafi and Gita **(c)** _____ only (hike) for a few hours when they came across a flock of sheep. It **(d)** _____ (watch) by an old shepherd who **(e)** _____ (lean) on a long thin stick. The old man **(f)** _____ (concentrate) on his flock and didn't notice their presence. Rafi sat down on a rock and Gita **(g)** _____ (walk) over to ask the shepherd for help when the massive dog, who **(h)** _____ (lie) at the shepherd's feet, suddenly stood up.

Vocabulary: nature

Vocabulary presentation

In all good stories, details of the setting are important so you need the right vocabulary to describe the natural surroundings.

5 What do these words from the story on pages 120–121 have in common?

> plane-tree   trunk
>
> branch   tree-stump

6 Match each group of words to a category in the box.

> river   mountain   plant
>
> beach   bird

a nest, feathers, beak, eggs

b ridge, peak, slope, face

c stream, waterfall, banks, estuary

d shore, shells, dunes, rock pools

e seed, petals, stalk, leaves

7 Choose the correct verb(s) to complete each sentence.

a A small lizard *crawled / slid* across the path.

b A blackbird was *landed / perched* on a small branch above her.

c The leaves on the tree *rustled / cracked* in the wind.

d Small waves *splashed / plunged* onto the beach.

e The river was *flying / flowing* fast and the rain was *draining / pouring* down.

Tip

When describing nature, use all the senses. Describe colours, sights, sounds, textures and smells.

Cohesion: connectives for narratives

Cohesion presentation

Use connectives to situate actions or events in time, sequence them, or move the action along.

8 Match the connectives with similar meanings.

a all at once		**i**	presently
b then		**ii**	when
c by the time		**iii**	suddenly
d before		**iv**	next
e soon		**v**	prior to

9 Which two connectives from the box below will you probably not use in a story to indicate time or sequence?

> as soon as   at this instant
>
> meanwhile   in essence
>
> instantly   at the same time
>
> as long as   for a while
>
> some time later   as

Guided writing

You have decided to enter a short story competition. Your local bookshop is giving away a set of books for the best story written by a young writer and the winning story will also be published on their website.

Write a story that includes the words 'He/She realised he/she was totally lost.'

Think/Plan

1 Work in pairs. Generate ideas for your stories. Answer the questions to help you.

   a Who is your main character?

   b Where is he/she? What is he/she doing there?

   c What are the consequences of your character getting lost?

   d What does he/she do about it?

   e What can you introduce to the story to heighten the tension?

Tip

You could use a spider diagram like the one on page 122 to organise your ideas.

2 Now think of ways to vary the tension in your story. In the story on pages 120–121, the tension is high at the beginning as the boy is running; then it lessens as he rests; then it rises again as he starts to run once more.

Plan your story. Think about the different settings you have to describe at each point as your character moves.

Useful language

Continuous tenses: *The sun was shining…, It was pouring with rain…, He/She was only wearing a light jacket…, He/She had been walking for several hours…, It had been raining for several hours when he/she…, He/She felt he/she was being watched…, He/She remembered his/her location was being tracked…*

Nature: *tree, branch, trunk, tree stump, mountain, ridge, peak, slope, face, river, stream, waterfall, banks, estuary, beach, shore, shells, dunes, rock pools, flowers, seeds, petals, stalk, leaves, bird, nest, feathers, beak, eggs, crawl, slide, perch, land, rustle, crack, splash, flow, pour down*

Connectives: *as, while, then, next, before, prior to, after, following, some time later, all at once, as soon as, at this instant, instantly, for a while, at the same time*

Write: the opening

In the opening of your story, you have two options:

   a start with the action – begin with high tension (your character panics on discovering he/she is lost)

   b give a detailed description of the setting and how your character moves around in it.

Here are some ideas:

a) action	b) description
hiking, walking – falls – hurts ankle	a forest – trees, dense vegetation, shadows
being chased by someone/ something – inner thoughts as he/she tries to escape	mountains – loose rocks, snow in the distance, a path
walking – hears sounds (wild animals?) – starts to run	beach – deserted, huge dunes, windy

Include some direct speech as your character talks/thinks to himself/herself about his/her situation.

Write: continue the story

If you chose option **a** above:

Change the rhythm and lessen the tension somehow.

For example, your character is out of breath and stops to rest – falls asleep?/hears animals?/takes shelter from the weather?

If you chose option **b** above:

Change the rhythm and introduce a sudden burst of action.

For example, something or someone is chasing him/her – a dog/a bear?

- Remember to maintain some mystery. Perhaps you don't want to identify why your character is where he/she is or who or what is chasing him/her.

- Continue the 'dialogue' with your character.

Write: finish the story

Now write the end of your story. This means another change in the rhythm/tension – less or more depending on the previous part.

Here are some ideas:

a He/She sees some signs of civilisation far away and heads in that direction.

b He/She decides it's too late in the day and prepares to spend the night out in the open air.

c In his/her desire to get away, he/she realises that he/she is completely lost.

d He/She is now confronted by whatever it was that was after him/her.

Things to remember when writing a story

- Keep some information from the reader to raise the reader's curiosity.

- Give your character a strong narrative voice.

- Generate interest in the main character – his/her situation, personality, etc.

- Build and lessen tension throughout the story.

- Describe the setting around the character in detail.

- Create obstacles that your characters have to overcome.

- Describe background actions using continuous tenses.

- Use connectives to link ideas, set the actions or events in time and move the action along.

Check your first draft

When you have finished writing, be your own editor.

- Let your story sit for a time – leave it and come back to it later with fresh eyes.

- Put yourself in the position of the reader.

- Check that you have varied the tension, building and lowering as necessary.

- Check that you a) haven't given everything away; and b) have given enough information to keep the reader's interest.

Now write a second draft of your story.

Peer assessment

Check your partner's story for consistency. Make sure it is told from the narrator's point of view.

Independent writing

Write about a character in a particular situation in a story of 350–400 words.

Choose *one* of these ideas or use your own.

- Stuck in a storm.
- Alone in a new village or city.
- He/She knew his/her life would never be the same again.

Include description, action and voice.

Follow these stages.

Stage 1 Generate ideas. Think about your character, the location where the story is set, the action, the character's voice.

Stage 2 Put your ideas into a plan, using a spider diagram.

- Nature and landscape/surroundings
- Emotions
- Physical condition

Stage 3 Write your story in paragraphs, following your plan. Use the checklist to make sure your story contains a powerful character.

Writer's checklist: stories

- Have you established and sustained your character?
- Do you create interest in your character from the beginning?
- Have you kept some information from the reader to heighten their interest?
- Have you combined the setting, situation or experience with the main story line?
- Have you given your character a strong voice?
- Have you used dialogue where needed to develop the character?
- Have you described the world around the character in detail?

Editor's checklist

Check

- that your ideas are organised into paragraphs
- your spelling and use of capital letters
- punctuation, especially commas and quotation marks
- the grammar is correct – continuous tenses.

Final draft

Once you have finished the scene for a story, swap it with someone else in your class and discuss the whole story. Then send it to your teacher.

Check your progress

I can:	Needs more work	Almost there	All done!
establish and sustain a character, point of view and voice			
create effect and purpose through a wide variety of sentence types			
create interest in the character and maintain it by withholding certain information			
make my story clear with the use of narrative connectives.			